Your Plan

for a

BALANCED

LIFE™

Your Plan *for a* BALANCED LIFE™

James M. Rippe, M.D.

THOMAS NELSON
Since 1798

NASHVILLE   DALLAS   MEXICO CITY   RIO DE JANEIRO   BEIJING

Published in Nashville, Tennessee, by Thomas Nelson. Thomas Nelson is a registered trademark of Thomas Nelson, Inc.

Thomas Nelson, Inc., titles may be purchased in bulk for educational, business, fund-raising, or sales promotional use. For information, please e-mail SpecialMarkets@ThomasNelson.com.

Your Plan for a Balanced Life, Balanced Life, Start Making Choices are trademarks of ConAgra Foods RDM, Inc.

Library of Congress Cataloging-in-Publication Data

Rippe, James M.
  Your plan for a balanced life / James M Rippe.
      p. cm.
  Includes bibliographical references and index.
  ISBN 978-1-4016-0392-2 *3-30-10*
  1. Nutrition—Popular works. 2. Exercise—Popular works. 3. Self-care, Health—Popular works. I. Title.
RA784.R54 2008
613.2—dc22

2007038647

Printed in the United States of America
08 09 10 11 RRD 5 4

This book is dedicated to Stephanie, Hart, Jaelin, Devon, and Jamie. You give my life balance, purpose, and meaning.

Table of Contents

Part 1 | The Benefits of a Balanced Life

Part 2 | Your Personalized Plan for a Balanced Life

Appendix

A Planning Tools

B Nutrition Tools

Acknowledgments

Many of the concepts presented in *Your Plan for a Balanced Life* are the result of years of hard work on the part of many talented individuals both at my research laboratory, Rippe Lifestyle Institute, and at my clinic, Rippe Health Assessment. I have been blessed to have incredible friends and colleagues throughout my adult life who have made major contributions to the work that I describe in this book. I am deeply grateful to these individuals who are too numerous to acknowledge by name.

While many individuals have made major contributions to the effort of producing this book, special thanks are due to Mary Abbott Waite, PhD. This is the seventh book project on which Mary Abbott Waite and I have collaborated. Mary Abbott continues to amaze me with her ability to take my manuscripts and organize, clarify, and enhance my words and thoughts. She does this with the wonderful and subtle skill of disappearing within my voice. Without Mary Abbott's formidable talents, deep commitment to all aspects of our collaboration, and enormous energy, books like the one that you are currently holding in your hands would not be possible. Mary Abbott is a wonderful professional, a gifted writer, and a close personal friend.

Much of the research that is referred to throughout this book has been conducted at Rippe Lifestyle Institute under the superb direction of my friend and colleague, Ted Angelopoulos, PhD, MPH. Ted wears many hats. He is the Director of Research at Rippe Lifestyle Institute and Rippe Health Assessment as well as Professor of Exercise Science at the University of Central Florida, where he also serves as the Research Director of our Center for Lifestyle Medicine. Ted's great skills and energy as well as his friendship are enormously important to me.

Our associate director of research, Linda Zukley, PhD, RN, CCRN, matches the energy and enthusiasm of Dr. Angelopoulos. She has great clinical skills and is a wonderful manager with deep dedication to the clinical research that we conduct at Rippe Lifestyle Institute. Drs. Angelopoulos and Zukley are supported by a team of nutritionists, exercise physiologists, and other support staff who do a magnificent job carrying out the daily research and putting the ideas that I discuss in this book into practice.

My clinical facility, Rippe Health Assessment, is guided by a wonderful team of physicians who deliver a high standard of medical care and caring that are the hallmarks of the Rippe Health Assessment experience. The clinical team is led by doctors Sherri Brooks, Sherry Novenstern, and Christie Edwards. Amy Stachnik does an outstanding job as the director of client services for RHA, and Hermino Alamo, MHA, RN, leads the team of exercise physiologists, nurses, nutritionists, and other support personnel who deliver the wonderful clinical and caring experience to every patient every day in our clinic.

Thanks are due to the science and nutrition teams at ConAgra Foods for many helpful thoughts and suggestions. Jim Astwood, PhD, vice president, scientific and regulatory affairs/nutrition research, quality and innovation, has been a great scientific colleague and friend. Patty Packard, MS, RD, Kristi Reimers, PhD, RD, Kasia Burton, RD, and their team spearheaded the effort to develop the meal plans and recipes found in *Your Plan for a Balanced Life*.

The executive and editorial teams at Thomas Nelson have been great supporters of this project and a pleasure to work with. Pamela

Clements, vice president and publisher, has been an early and avid supporter of this entire project. David Dunham, senior vice president, also supported this project from its earliest days. Geoffrey Stone, editor in chief, has provided wise counsel and direction during every phase of this project. Emily Prather has demonstrated great skill as the editor.

A special thanks to my literary agent on this project, Lee Hough, who has enthusiastically supported the project and handled numerous details.

I am fortunate to be able to lead an academic effort at the University of Central Florida to establish the Center for Lifestyle Medicine at UCF. This has been made possible through the strong support of the president of UCF, Dr. John Hitt, who is a true visionary and a great friend.

I am also deeply grateful to the thousands of research subjects and patients who have come through my clinical research organization, Rippe Lifestyle Institute, and my clinic, Rippe Health Assessment, over the past two decades. Their experiences have taught me and inspired me to become both a better physician and a better human being. I draw upon the wisdom of their progress toward balanced, healthy living in stories throughout this book but have changed their names and condensed or combined experiences to illustrate key points and to protect their privacy.

No literary project would be conceivable without my superb editorial director, Elizabeth Grady, who has ably coordinated all editorial activities for my organization for more than twenty years. Beth has a great energy, phenomenal organizational skills, and a deep passion for excellence that drives these projects to completion.

My executive assistant, Carol Moreau, does a superb job managing my complicated and busy career, which consists of many different aspects, including research, patient care, public speaking, and consulting. Carol is one of the most organized and competent people I have ever met and probably knows more about my life than I do. My executive assistant and office manager, Becky Cotton-Hess, at our research organization in Florida, the Rippe Lifestyle Research Institute of Florida, supports my efforts with great skill, caring, and competence. I am deeply grateful for the hard work and dedication that they have displayed on this and many other projects.

Finally, my dear wife, Stephanie Hart Rippe, supports every aspect of my life and provides constant love and encouragement. She manages a very complex home life that involves not only me but also our four beautiful, energetic daughters, Hart, Jaelin, Devon, and Jamie, who fill my heart with joy. These five women together comprise the "Rippe Women" and make me determined always to be the best that I can be while informing the daily struggle for me to balance both family and professional aspects of my life.

JMR
Boston, MA

A Question of Balance

Most of us would like to have better balance in our lives. We'd like to balance family, work, leisure, relaxation, fitness, and nutrition. We like feeling in control of our lives, and we genuinely would like to make choices that promote our health and quality of life.

Most of us know the basic things that we need to do to be healthier and happier. We know that we should try to eat better. We know that we should try to be more physically active. We know that it is important to have time for our family and friends and to decrease our stress in a hectic, complicated, and tense world. But most of us experience a frustrating gap between what we would like to do and getting it done. The realities of busy lives with multiple commitments too often get in our way. We all seem to have "so much to do, so little time to do it."

I see this in my own life, balancing a career and home life with my wife and four young daughters. And I've seen it in thousands of patients in my clinic at Rippe Health Assessment and at our research facility, Rippe Lifestyle Institute. Many people have come to us with their health and lives wildly out of balance. And the most important thing we do is help these women and men find ways to achieve that elusive balance.

The foundation for the best possible quality of life is a balanced lifestyle that includes sound nutrition to provide health and energy, activity to keep your body's systems conditioned and your muscles strong and flexible, and well-being strategies to help you manage stress and promote emotional and spiritual well-being. *Your Plan for a Balanced Life* can be the key to getting control of your life.

Balance Adds Strength

An equilateral triangle symbolizes balance—it is nature's strongest geometric shape. It can also represent three fundamental and equal requirements for achieving a balanced life:

- ▲ Nutrition—healthy food choices that enrich your life
- ▲ Activity—keeping your body moving
- ▲ Well-Being—finding time for relaxation and spending time with friends and family

If all three sides are of equal length, a triangle is strong and balanced. But if you "unbalance" it by shortening one of its sides, you weaken the whole structure. Similarly, if you neglect or overemphasize any of the three fundamentals of your health—nutrition, activity, or well-being—you will throw your life out of balance.

These three fundamentals of sound nutrition, activity, and well-being will form the core of your plan. Let's take the analogy one step farther and bring it to life like this:

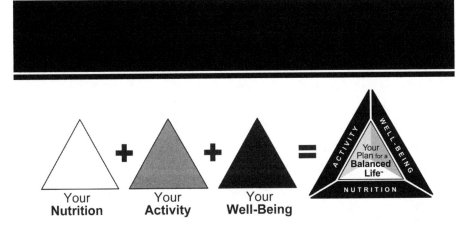

Your **Nutrition** + Your **Activity** + Your **Well-Being** = ACTIVITY · WELL-BEING · Your Plan for a **Balanced Life** · NUTRITION

See the difference? A triangle is flat, two-dimensional. Adding you—your goals and choices—to the strength of balanced nutrition, activity, and well-being turns the triangle into a solid 3-D structure: a personalized, dynamic plan for achieving a balanced life.

You are the most important factor in this pyramid. You make the choices to create and carry out a plan that works for you and your family because it's tailored to your needs and circumstances. *Your Plan for a Balanced Life* will provide the concepts, strategies, tools, and tips you'll need.

Partnering for Your Success

This book will offer you practical strategies and tips, and from these you can choose what will work for you and your family to help balance your daily life in three areas: nutrition, activity, and well-being. You'll build on this plan, one practice or choice at a time.

I often say to patients or research participants that to succeed in improving health and quality of life, we must form a true partnership. True partners work together to figure out the best strategies, while recognizing each other's strengths and weaknesses. This program will analyze your strengths and weaknesses and will help you build a plan to achieve balance in your life.

You'll also find a helpful Web site at StartMakingChoices.com that will provide you with free information, encouragement, and feedback.

This Web site was created by professionals from ConAgra Foods, Inc. along with me and my research laboratory. The Web site features a Balanced Life™ Planner with daily nutrition, activity, and well-being guidelines that you can customize to meet your personal balance needs. In the Nutrition area, you can customize meal plans, and you can access a food log that will automatically analyze your daily nutritional intake. In the Activity section, you can custom design a daily exercise plan, and you can log your daily activities. This section also offers tools that help you quickly calculate your BMI (body mass index), target heart rate, and recommended daily caloric intake. StartMakingChoices.com even offers well-being tools like suggestions for strengthening your relationships with friends and family, managing stress, and making time for yourself. You can use this Web site along with *Your Plan for a Balanced Life*, or use this book as a stand-alone guide.

Using This Book

Your Plan for a Balanced Life has three major parts:

Part One, "The Benefits of a Balanced Life," includes a quick overview of the benefits of a balanced lifestyle—and some of the risks you run if your life lacks balance. Then comes an overview of how you will personalize your plan to meet your needs and those of your family.

Part Two, "Your Personalized Plan for a Balanced Life," takes you

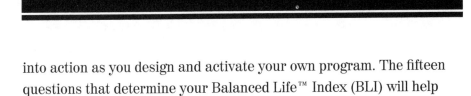

into action as you design and activate your own program. The fifteen questions that determine your Balanced Life™ Index (BLI) will help you get a good baseline assessment of where you are in nutrition, activity, and well-being. The BLI also serves as a great tool to track your progress. Using your score, you move to personal goal-setting and planning. Then we identify the key components of balancing nutrition, activity, and well-being in your life, and we provide practical strategies for incorporating these components into your daily plan. We also discuss how to use this

This program will analyze your strengths and weaknesses and build a plan to help you achieve balance in your life.

book's many tools, such as the two-week meal plan or the twenty-week walking program.

The appendices, "Easy-to-Use Tools to Balance Your Life," give you techniques and tools to carry out your plan. You'll find delicious, easy-to-make recipes, a two-week meal plan, and many more tools.

At the end of the book you'll find additional recommended resources and references.

Let's Get Started

An ancient Chinese proverb reminds us that the longest journey begins with a single step. If you're reading this book, chances are you want to start taking those steps to achieve more balance, joy, meaning, and health. *Your Plan for a Balanced Life* can help you achieve just that.

Part 1
The
Benefits of a
Balanced
Life

The Benefits of a Balanced Life

I remember the day Sharon plopped down on the seat beside me in my research lab. She was clutching a newspaper ad seeking participants for a new research trial that would study the results of a twelve-week program of low-fat nutrition, walking, and group support designed to help people lose weight while maintaining lean muscle mass and metabolism.

"I'm tired," she said. "Physically tired and emotionally tired. I'm tired of feeling out of control, I'm tired of being overweight, and I'm plain tired of being tired. I'd like to take more time with family and friends, but when I'm not working, I'm too tired."

Sharon was one of the best nurses in our coronary care unit, where we had collaborated caring for very ill patients for nearly a decade.

"I've tried every diet in the book," she said. "From grapefruit to no carb, from low-fat to high protein—I've tried it—and failed. You can spend just so long in food prison. And even though my job is very active with lots of walking, I just don't maintain the weight I want."

Sharon went on to tell me that in nursing school and just after, she had felt on top of things—fit and a healthy weight, eager to take on the world. But as she started her nursing career and married life, she slipped out of balance. She worked long hours at a stress-filled job, managed a new home, entertained, and ate dinner out with her husband three or four times a week. With each pregnancy, Sharon put on a reasonable amount of weight, but after each birth she lost only part of that weight. By age forty, she was thirty-five pounds overweight—not "a lot," but at 20 to 25 percent above her healthy weight range, it affected her energy and increased her health risks.

"I'm tired of it," Sharon said. "I want to get back in control."

In the random draw, Sharon was chosen for the trial. Her baseline health and fitness measures were no surprise. She was overweight, poorly conditioned, and anxious. Her BMI was 27.5 (which indicates an unhealthy weight); her body fat was 34 percent; her aerobic capacity was below average, and she was eating 2,570 calories a day, too much for her body size and activity level—with 42 percent of calories from fat (the recommended maximum is 30-35 percent). Psychological testing indicated that Sharon was anxious and mildly depressed and lacked confidence in her physical ability. She had average scores on her perceived quality of life, which matched her own perception. She was overweight, not fit or strong, and unhappy with her lifestyle.

Balance grows from the synergistic power of sound nutrition, activity, and well-being.

But she knew that both her quality of life and her health and fitness would benefit if she could regain control and get many aspects of her lifestyle in balance.

Thousands of studies have confirmed and expanded our knowledge of the benefits every person can derive from achieving the balance that grows from the synergistic power of sound nutrition, activity, and well-being. Let's look at the benefits that awaited Sharon—and that await you as you begin to find balance in your life.

Why We Thrive on Balance

The living human body is an intricate and remarkable organism with many interdependent systems. When all the body's systems function as they were designed to do, we enjoy good health. Truly good health—the health you deserve—equips you to face the challenges and delights of your life with vigor and competence.

To function well and to maintain health, your body needs:

▲ balanced nutrients to support its varied systems, from your heart and blood vessels, lungs, and nerves to your muscles and bones, digestive tract, metabolic gland, and beyond
▲ physical activity to keep these systems fit and well-conditioned
▲ enough relaxation and activity to relieve stress and promote spiritual health

Just as we desire balance in our lives, our bodies are designed to respond or adapt to sustain a "state of balance," called *homeostasis*.

Positive Changes Work Together

Everything you do to improve your life will help, whether it's taking a few minutes a day to meditate, choosing fruit for dessert, or walking around the block every evening. But what you may not realize is that these steps are synergistic—their effect combined is greater than the sum of the impact of each separate step.

For instance, eating more whole grains, fruits, and vegetables and fewer foods rich in saturated fat will lower your risks for many diseases. And if you increase your activity level to thirty total minutes a day of moderate to brisk activity, you will lower your risk factors for many diseases. But if you improve your eating habits *and* increase your activity levels, the benefits of the two changes will be far greater.

Now, throw in the added support of stress management and other well-being components and you can reach a whole new level of health and happiness.

How Small Changes Can Affect Your Life

You may think that little changes such as daily walking or eating a healthy breakfast don't do much—but besides improving your day-to-day health and energy levels, they can help you live longer. A 2004 study reported in the Journal of the American Medical Association followed approximately 2,300 European men and women from eleven countries, ages seventy to ninety, for more than ten years.[1] The results were striking: Those who (1) ate a diet that emphasized fruits, vegetables, whole grains, and olive oil; (2) were physically active; (3) never smoked or had quit smoking at least fifteen years previously; and (4) used alcohol moderately had a 50 percent lower risk of death from disease and illness.

Another study involving healthy Americans ages seventy to eighty-two found that active energy expenditure was positively and progressively associated with a lower risk of death from disease and illness.[2] Older adults who practice such well-being strategies as staying connected with others and sharing their

If You Want to Get Started Right Now

If you absolutely want to get started right now, go for it. Here are several options:

▲ **Option 1. Start the Balanced Walking Program.** All you need is a good pair of walking shoes and comfortable clothing. The Balanced Walking Program on page 87 starts with a ten-minute walk three days a week, whenever you can fit it into your schedule. Tip for success: Write your walk sessions in your schedule (lunchtime, after work, whenever fits) as you would any appointment. Once you start walking, turn back to this chapter and continue to make a complete plan for balance, including building optimal eating and well-being strategies into your life.

▲ **Option 2. Sign up for a personal plan on StartMakingChoices.com.** By registering at our companion Web site, www.StartMakingChoices.com, you can take our assessment survey online and the program will automatically generate a balanced meal plan and any activity plans you select. But start with only a walking program or meal plan or both—you'll add other programs such as flexibility and strength training as you progress. We'll tell you how in chapter 7.

▲ **Option 3. Launch our basic plan for balance.** In chapter 9 you'll find a template for a basic plan that starts with nutrition, using the two-week meal plan, and gradually adds the walking program, well-being steps, and other activity plans. But to create an individualized plan and to optimize your chances of success, turn back here to keep reading and working with the chapters on nutrition, activity, and well-being.

talents with the community also may enjoy greater average longevity.

The Many Benefits of a Balanced Life

The benefits of a balanced life are too many to list, but here are a few:

Reduces disease risks. The strategies you'll find in this book can help lower your risk factors for heart disease, stroke, high blood pressure, diabetes, some cancers, and other chronic diseases—all are directly affected by lifestyle choices. Most major chronic diseases share many of the same risk factors, which may be triggered by poor eating habits, lack of activity, being overweight, and not handling life's stresses well.

Helps with day-to-day activities. Functional fitness is the ability to comfortably carry out all the activities of daily life. Strong muscles and good balance contribute to mobility; eating calcium-rich foods, and participating in weight-bearing activity all help build and maintain healthy bones; good food and staying active can improve joint health. The list goes on!

Controls stress. Something as simple as walking around the block every morning makes it easier to cope with stressors. Research suggests that physical activity actually protects cells from an inflammatory reaction triggered by your body's "stress system." Techniques that tap the mind-body connection, such as relaxation methods and anger and guilt management skills, can also help you handle stress positively. And eating foods rich in antioxidants, such as fruits and vegetables, may help to protect against physical damage from stress.

Enhances mood and keeps you sharp. Regular activity helps to prevent depression and anxiety. And evidence is mounting that balanced nutrition and activity may also keep your mind sharp for those extra years of longevity. Activity, in particular, may help to preserve cognitive function and possibly prevent or delay the onset of Alzheimer's disease or other types of dementia.[3]

> *Regular activity helps to prevent depression and anxiety.*

Supports healthy weight. A balanced approach to living lets you enjoy food while maintaining or reaching a healthy weight. This book will tell you how to satisfy hunger with nutrient-dense foods, and it will coach you into plans that will help maintain and build lean muscle mass. And we'll help you find well-being strategies to pamper or reward yourself—without eating!

Makes you look better, too. Healthy lifestyle choices and a sense of balance can make you feel and look better. Well-conditioned muscles, a spring in your step, and a spark of enthusiasm in your eye are attractive and winning at any age. Drinking plenty of water and eating a variety of nutritious foods helps keep your skin looking fresh and healthy.

The Choice Is Yours

These are some major benefits that await you! I have been privileged to observe and help thousands of people make changes in their lives to improve balance and health. By using this book to make a plan that fits your needs and realities, you can succeed, too. After all, these are not new strategies; they have been validated by time and success stories like Sharon's.

After her baseline evaluation, Sharon reviewed the nutrition and walking program and structured goals that had been created for her. She took fire. At the end of the twelve weeks, she had surpassed her goals. She had lost eighteen pounds, and her walking program had helped her build lean muscle mass. Her body fat had dropped to 25 percent and her aerobic capacity had expanded 20 percent. Her fat intake had dropped to 28 percent of total energy consumed, which is within the recommended range.

Most important to Sharon, she was no longer tired. "My energy and confidence are higher than they've ever been in my life," she exulted. Six months later, Sharon had reached her goal of a healthy weight for her size and kept on walking. "I couldn't live without it," she said. By achieving nutritional and activity balance in her life, Sharon had also tapped into a source of energy that helped her balance other areas of her life.

You can do it, too.

Getting off Track–and Back On

Judith and Richard never met each other. But they were sailing blithely along in the same boat, wondering whether they had enough gas to reach their destination—while unknown to them, their boat had sprung multiple leaks and was taking on water.

Both of them were at Rippe Health Assessment for a comprehensive health assessment, and both had a similar view of their health status: basically good but in need of some adjustments. In her early forties, Judith was a successful senior human resources executive for a large company and the mother of two teenagers. Although she judged that she was too sedentary and probably had put on too many pounds, she felt fine and energetic.

Making a contribution to his Fortune 500 company's bottom line absorbed Richard's focus and energy. He loved his work and spent long hours at his desk, in meetings, and on airplanes "getting the job done." That's all he had time for, in his view. Richard had no idea how risky his out-of-balance lifestyle was.

Judith had not really grasped her risks, either. As she had coasted into inactivity, Judith had gained a pound or two a year. She tried to eat "sensibly" but didn't look closely at nutritional balance. To her surprise, she found that her fasting blood sugar was high, placing her at risk for diabetes. Blood pressure readings of 140/88 placed her in borderline stage 1 high blood pressure. Her cardiovascular fitness, measured by a treadmill test, was below average, and her total cholesterol and triglycerides were both high—all risk factors for heart disease. A CT scan showed minor calcification in two of three coronary arteries, early indicators of heart disease.

Judith agreed whole-heartedly that it was time to make some changes.

I had a tougher sell convincing Richard that he must take steps to take control and balance his lifestyle. Richard's custom was to eat whatever he wanted whenever he had time to do it, except for planned business meals. Many of the latter were rich meals at fancy restaurants. The most activity he got was walking through airport concourses, where he took shuttle carts whenever possible. Richard believed that doing deals provided most of the pleasure he needed. His test results clearly showed the risks he was running. More than one hundred pounds above healthy weight, Richard had early diabetes and high blood pressure. Tests of his coronary arteries revealed significant narrowing caused by the fatty deposits of coronary heart disease. I warned Richard that unless he made some immediate changes, the probability of his being able—or even around—to do business in the future was shrinking steadily.

The good news—for both Judith and Richard and for you—is that it takes only modest, consistent effort to reclaim balance and health.

> *It takes only modest, consistent effort to reclaim balance and health.*

Being a Little out of Balance Can = Big Trouble

Like Judith and Richard, most of us drift slowly out of balance and into trouble. None of us makes a conscious decision to start taking those small steps that eventually risk our health. They just "happen" while we're busy with work and family and other interests. As a result, many of us have slipped into risky behaviors and may have developed risk factors for chronic disease.

Scary statistics are easy to find:

▲ Lifestyle practices contribute to at least seven of the ten leading causes of death in the U.S.: heart disease, cancer, stroke, chronic respiratory disease, accidents, diabetes, and Alzheimer's disease.[1]

▲ About three-fourths of Americans do not engage in enough activity to improve their health—and two in five get no regular activity at all.[2]

▲ Only about one-third of U.S. adults eat two or more servings of fruit daily and even fewer eat three or more servings of vegetables, the minimum recommendations for good nutrition.[3]

▲ Roughly two-thirds of American adults are overweight or obese: 70.5 percent of men and 61.6 percent of women.[4]

▲ More than half of us are concerned about how much stress we have in our everyday lives, and work significantly affects stress levels in 62 percent of Americans.[5]

We're too sedentary, we don't eat well, we are stressed out—and all this is draining our energy and making us sick. You probably already know what many of us are doing wrong in our eating: eating too few fruits, vegetables, and whole grains; not getting enough calcium; and eating too much saturated fat and cholesterol-rich foods—and more calories than we need!

Being sedentary contributes to fatigue and weight gain, can shrink and weaken your muscles, increases your risk for heart problems and other diseases, increases anxiety and stress, and even weakens your immune system.

Without enough time for relaxation or fun, built-up stress can cause fatigue, lack of energy, irritability, anger, or sleeplessness; contribute to high blood pressure, heart problems, and depression; weaken the immune system; and cause a host of other problems.

A balanced life is looking better and better, right? All of these things creeep up on us, little by little, and it requires a well-planned effort to make changes. In the chapters to come, we'll help you tackle all of these issues, and come up with a sustainable plan to make you happier and healthier—and keep you that way the rest of your life.

Reclaiming Balance

Some of us have given up trying to maintain a healthy lifestyle. We think to ourselves, *Que sera, sera*—whatever will be, will be.

Every potential danger can be turned around by making the right choices for nutrition, activity, and well-being.

But every risk factor, every potential danger mentioned in this chapter can be turned around by making the right choices for nutrition, activity, and well-being. Judith and Richard, with the help of our clinic's caring professionals, identified and acted on the right choices for them.

Judith realized that she had had the most difficulty with "mindless" food choices. She sat down with one of our nutritionists to make a food plan that would fit her needs and her schedule; she made follow-up appointments with the nutritionist for additional support and opportunities to fine-tune her nutrition goals and strategies. She began a regular walking program; the simple training calendar balanced her need to start slowly with her desire to see some benefit as quickly as possible. When I saw Judith a year later for her annual evaluation, I applauded. She looked a decade younger, and she'd hit her health goals. With the loss of about thirty pounds, her blood pressure had dropped. Her blood sugar had fallen into the normal range, as had her cholesterol and triglycerides. Judith was enthusiastic about her improved health and energy. With great pleasure, she announced that she'd dropped three dress sizes and would look terrific for her daughter's upcoming wedding.

With Richard, we took a different approach. Although he was finally convinced that for his health's sake he needed to make some immediate changes, Richard wasn't particularly optimistic about his ability to act on his good intentions when his business consumed his concentration and time. So for Richard we made a "business case" for change and helped him lay out a "business plan" to fit his strategic goals for health balance into his passion for business.

When I saw Richard a year later, he had reached his weight loss goal and doubled his cardiovascular fitness. His high blood pressure and diabetes had disappeared, and his cholesterol levels had improved dramatically. Five years later, Richard has made his plan for balance part of his way of doing business and has maintained all his health gains.

Both Judith and Richard reclaimed balance in their lives—they worked to assess where they were; made a specific, personal plan to reach their goals; and then carried them out.

With the help of this book, so can you.

ACTIVITY

WELL-BEING

Your
Plan for a
**Balanced
Life**™

NUTRITION

Ready to Succeed?
Prepare Yourself for Change

It may help to jot down some reasons you want to change. Some of your reasons and hopes may be similar to these, voiced by others who wanted to change their lives:

▲ *I'd like to find a permanent way to live that's healthy.*
▲ *I often eat for convenience rather than for maintaining a healthy weight.*
▲ *I need to stop putting my needs last.*
▲ *I'd like a physical activity routine that fits my life.*
▲ *I need a plan that works for everyone in the family so I don't have to do one thing for myself and different things for them.*
▲ *I want to manage my health condition and lower the risks for other problems.*

In an old airline commercial, a frazzled passenger complains that he is in Des Moines but his luggage has gone to Dubuque. If you launch your plan toward an unknown destination, it may not be where you want to go. So take some time to plan. Approach your plan as if you were planning a long-anticipated trip or a dream addition to your home. After all, this is *your life* we're talking about.

Before you read on, take a few moments to jot down your primary reasons or goals for seeking greater balance in your life. What would you like to get out of this book?

1. _____

_____

2. _____

_____

3. _____

_____

4. _____

_____

5. _____

_____

If you listed more than three reasons or goals, put a star by the three most important to you.

Empowering Yourself to Succeed

We all intuitively know that our minds can be either a powerful ally or an impediment to accomplishing our goals. Having the proper perspective can help you achieve the kind of balance, happiness, and meaning you desire. Conversely, if you plunge blindly into action, you can create mental barriers that set you up for failure.

How can you build a foundation for success?

The Five Stages of Changes

Change—even minor change—is difficult. But I have seen thousands of people make powerful changes for the better in their lives. What helped them succeed was understanding how change happens: they recognized that change is a continuous process, which occurs in stages.[1]

Not Ready Yet

Maintaining a Good Thing For Life!

Taking Action

Preparing for Action

Thinking about it

Stage 1. Not ready. You're not ready yet to think about change; the idea may even make you cross or angry.

Stage 2. Thinking about it. You have identified a change you want to make. You begin to think how you might do it, and doing it seems more attractive than not doing it.

Stage 3. Preparing for action. You begin to make concrete plans for how to go about making the change.

Making small, incremental changes over many weeks, months, and years is the way to establish new patterns that will stick in your life.

Stage 4. Taking action. You put your plan into motion, and you may ask for or arrange support. You keep practicing.

Stage 5. Maintaining. By practicing, the change has become a habit. Depending on the nature of the change and your personal realities, making the change an established habit may take weeks or months. And you'll need to have a strategy in mind for restarting if you slip back into old habits.

You've picked up this book, so you're already past the first stage!

Slow and Steady Wins the Race

You may have heard the story of the tortoise and the hare: The hare blasts off the starting line, running as fast as he can and laughing at the slow tortoise. The tortoise pays no attention but keeps moving, step after step. Meanwhile, the hare takes a nap. The tortoise keeps chugging along until he chugs past the foolish hare and over the finish line.

Many people try to achieve balance in their lives in a very unbalanced way! They decide to make big changes in their life and don't recognize that making small, incremental changes over many weeks, months, and years is the way to establish new patterns that will stick in your life. Remember the victorious tortoise and give yourself credit for making slow and steady changes toward your goal.

Accept That You Are Worthy of Change

I have often wondered why so many of us know what we should be doing to improve our lives, yet we don't do it. We say that we are busy. We say that we are going to put off change for another day. We say that others need our attention more.

What holds us back? I think we feel that we are not worth the effort. If we feel unworthy, then we give up almost before we've begun.

If you have this sense of unworthiness, I need to say something just to you. If you are alive and breathing on the planet, you are worthy of the best that life has to offer. Your dreams and goals are as valid and important as any other person's—no more, no less. It's time for you to accept your value. Change is possible, and

For the greatest gain, you must trust that family and friends will offer support if you share your goals.

you have enormous power to achieve it. The first step is to accept as a birthright that you are worthy of making the effort.

The Three Factors of Success

There are three things you'll need while taking control of your life: trust, courage, and consistency.

Trust

Achieving balance requires trust—trust in yourself and trust in others. You must trust that you are capable of seeing what you need to do and taking steps to do it. Fortunately, every small step you complete strengthens your conviction that you can succeed and spurs you on.

But achieving balance is not a solo effort. For the greatest gain, you must trust that family and friends will offer support if you share your goals. In my practice, I have encountered many women who've resisted taking a twenty- or thirty-minute daily walk because they felt that taking that time away from their family was selfish. When they shared their goals and hopes with their husbands and families, in most cases not only were their loved ones supportive, but in many instances they wanted to walk too.

Occasionally, some people close to you may have issues and problems of their own that they can't overcome. If that happens, just trust yourself, and quietly reach out to other friends.

Courage

It takes courage to look closely at your life and assess those areas that you want to change. If you have been sedentary, it takes courage to start exercising regularly. If you have gained twenty or thirty pounds, it takes courage to say to yourself—let alone to those around you—that you are going to lose this excess weight.

A man I'll call Mike wanted badly to get in better shape; he felt tired and pudgy. He had a training calendar for a walking program much like the Balanced Walking Program you'll find later in this book. It started with a ten-minute walk. But he was embarrassed to admit publicly that he needed to exercise. He shuddered to think of himself in shorts and shoes "panting and sweating" around the neighborhood.

Here's How It Works

To use this program, here's what you'll do:

▲ **Assess where you are.** Pinpointing your current status as precisely as possible helps identify your goals and the right strategies and activities to help you reach them. The Balanced Life Index (BLI) survey in the next chapter will help you assess your current life balance in nutrition, activity, and well-being. If your family (or another family member) is joining you in creating a plan, they also should take the BLI.

▲ **Set and prioritize major goals.** Using the BLI score and any other tools (such as exercise and meal plans) you choose in later chapters, you'll identify your goals for your plan and at least three major goals for the areas of nutrition, activity, and well-being. Then you'll prioritize these goals to help build your specific plan.

▲ **Identify your needs for balance.** The chapters on nutrition, activity, and well-being are packed with facts, strategies, techniques, and tips. You'll return to these chapters often to refresh ideas and choose additional steps. As you read through each chapter, think about the goals you've identified and mark things that address those goals. Treat this read-through as a creative shopping trip—the sky's the limit!

▲ **Creating and acting on your plan.** Time to act. You'll identify your specific priority goals and strategies. You'll also identify tools to use, such as the walking program or the two-week meal plan. Your Program Calendar will let you see exactly what you want to do and when you should be doing it. We'll also show you how to use the programs on StartMakingChoices.com.

START MAKING CHOICES.com

▲ **Maintaining progress: reassess, reward, and renew.** The greatest secret to successfully implementing your plan is . . . keep going no matter what! Success is often determined by simple doggedness. This plan will give you tangible feedback and help you keep going . . . no matter what!

But he'd made up his mind to start. When the day he'd set came, he opened his front door and took his first steps. It was midnight, and pitch black. For the first eight weeks of his program, he walked at night. But he didn't miss a session. By week nine, he felt fitter, more energetic, and proud. He switched to daylight walks.

Understand that reaching your goals will call on your courage—but you can do it.

Consistency

Change occurs most easily and effectively when you consistently practice the strategies you've chosen. That's why it's important to choose changes that fit with your current daily habits and practices. Many people start off enthusiastically and full of good intentions, but soon give up. Two factors may contribute to this failure: doing too much too fast, and not rewarding yourself enough. When you make small changes, it's often hard to see your progress. I liken it to a parent's perception of a growing child. Because I see my daughters daily, I may not notice how much they have changed over a two-month period until a grandparent arrives and comments on their growth.

Heading toward the Next Steps

As you consider the goals and specific changes required to achieve better balance in your life, return to this chapter as needed to remind yourself that your attitudes and mental framework can become a great strength. If you understand that change is a process, that slow and steady wins the race, that you are worthy of enjoying balance, and that you can establish the trust, courage, and consistency necessary for change, you will have turned your mind into a powerful ally.

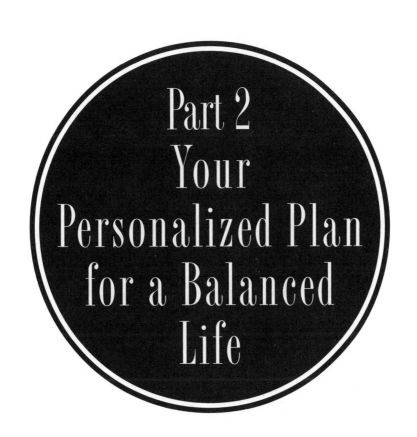

Part 2
Your
Personalized Plan
for a Balanced
Life

Assessing Your Status with the Balanced Life Index

It's time to determine your Balanced Life Index to get a clear estimate of your current status. The BLI will give you a great starting point to understand your areas of strength and weakness in nutrition, activity, and well-being. It's not a test, just a great way to see if your life is balanced and to take a first step to achieving more balance in your life.

The BLI also will allow you to track your progress regularly (we recommend weekly). You can use the paper version or take it on StartMakingChoices.com. As you begin to make changes in your life and update your personal online log, the Internet version will automatically update your BLI score for you. If you use the pencil and paper form, you can use the blank copy of the BLI on pages 26-30 to make extra copies, so you can update the BLI to track your progress in the weeks and months to come.

The Genesis of the BLI Questions

The nutrition questions in the BLI are derived from recommended eating patterns from the 2005 Dietary Guidelines for Americans. The Guidelines are updated every five years based on recommendations from an expert panel that considers hundreds of research studies. These recommendations form the basis of MyPyramid, the food guide our nutrition plan incorporates.

The activity questions are based on recommendations from Centers for Disease Control and Prevention and the American College of Sports Medicine and draw from validated questionnaires that have been used internationally to assess levels of activity and relate them to health.

The well-being questionnaire is derived from an extensive review of the research on various well-being concepts conducted by my team at Rippe Lifestyle Institute. This information is based on concepts that my research and clinical staff have used with thousands of patients for their annual health evaluations or as part of the various research studies we have conducted.

The Balanced Life Survey

To complete the survey, all you need are a comfortable chair, a pen or pencil (or a computer), and five minutes of time. Answer the questions by circling the appropriate answer. (To take the survey online, click on the Balanced Life Survey at StartMakingChoices.com.)

NUTRITION		
Question	**Responses**	**Score**
1. About how many cups of fruit did you eat today or on an average day this week?	a) $\frac{1}{4}$ to $\frac{1}{2}$ cup b) 1 to 1 $\frac{1}{2}$ cups	20 30

Question	Responses	Score
Examples of 1 cup: * • 1 cup of fresh fruit, or canned fruit • 1 cup of 100 percent fruit juice • $\frac{1}{2}$ cup of dried fruit	c) 2 to 2 $\frac{1}{2}$ cups d) 3 to 3 $\frac{1}{2}$ cups e) Don't know or less than $\frac{1}{4}$ cup	70 70 10
2. About how many cups of vegetables did you eat today or on an average day this week? Examples of 1 cup: * • 1 cup of raw or cooked vegetables • 1 cup of vegetable juice • 2 cups of raw leafy greens	a) $\frac{1}{4}$ to $\frac{1}{2}$ cup b) 1 to 1 $\frac{1}{2}$ cups c) 2 to 2 $\frac{1}{2}$ cups d) 3 to 3 $\frac{1}{2}$ cups e) Don't know or less than $\frac{1}{4}$ cup	20 30 70 70 10
3. About how many cups of milk, or foods made from fluid milk such as yogurt or cheese, did you eat today or on an average day this week? Examples of 1 cup: * • 1 cup of milk or yogurt • 1 $\frac{1}{2}$ ounces of natural cheese • 2 ounces of processed cheese	a) $\frac{1}{2}$ cup b) 1 cup c) 2 cups d) 3 cups e) Don't know or less than $\frac{1}{2}$ cup	20 30 50 70 10
4. On an average day, about how many ounces of your grain choices are whole grain? Examples of one ounce: * • 1 slice of 100 percent whole-grain bread • $\frac{1}{2}$ cup cooked oatmeal, bulgar, brown rice, or whole-grain pasta • 1 cup whole-grain ready-to-eat breakfast cereal • 1 whole-grain corn 6" tortilla • 3 cups popcorn	a) $\frac{1}{2}$ to 1 ounce b) 2 ounces c) 3 ounces d) 4 to 5 ounces e) Don't know or less than $\frac{1}{2}$ ounce	20 30 70 70 10
5. About how many of your daily food choices are foods such as candy, sweetened beverages, desserts, salty snacks, alcoholic beverages, or fatty foods?	a) 2 or fewer a day b) 3 a day c) 4 a day d) 5 or more a day e) Don't know	70 50 30 10 10

Nutrition Score *(Add questions 1-5 in this section)* _____

* See page 161 for additional examples

ACTIVITY

Question	Responses	Score
1. On a typical day, how much total incidental* activity did you accumulate? For example, if you walked the dog for 10 minutes, walked at lunch for 10 minutes, and cleaned the house for 10 minutes, you accumulated 30 minutes. Other examples are physical activity at work, walking to and from the car, climbing stairs, playing with kids, walking while shopping, gardening, or mowing the lawn.	a) Less than 10 minutes b) 10 to 19 minutes c) 20 to 29 minutes d) 30 to 44 minutes e) 45+ minutes	10 20 30 50 70
2. How many days in the past seven did you perform planned physical activities such as walking, jogging, or swimming?	a) None b) 1 day c) 2 days d) 3 days e) 4 or more days	10 20 30 50 70
3. How many days in the last seven did you strength train such as lifting weights, doing calisthenics, or practicing Pilates?	a) None b) 1 day c) 2 days d) 3 days e) 4 days	10 20 30 50 70
4. How many days in the last seven did you do flexibility exercises such as a stretching program, yoga classes, or tai chi?	a) None b) Only stretching as warm up and cool down to other activities such as a walking program c) 1 to 2 days d) 3 days e) 4+ days	10 20 30 50 70

Incidental activity is any activity besides your planned physical activity during the day where you are moving at a moderate pace.

Question	Responses	Score
5. How much time on an average day do you spend watching TV, using the computer recreationally, chatting on the phone or text messaging, playing video games, or otherwise sitting or lounging?	a) Less than 1 hour b) 1 hour c) 2 hours d) 3 hours e) 4 or more hours	70 50 30 20 10

Activity Score *(Add answers 1-5 in this section)* _____

WELL-BEING

Question	Responses	Score
1. In general, how satisfied are you with the amount and quality of time you take for yourself?	a) Very satisfied b) Satisfied c) Neither satisfied nor dissatisfied d) Dissatisfied e) Very dissatisfied	60 50 30 20 10
2. In general, how satisfied are you with the time you spend with family and/or friends doing such things as conversing, eating meals together, spending leisure time at home, or enjoying events away from home?	a) Very satisfied b) Satisfied c) Neither satisfied nor dissatisfied d) Dissatisfied e) Very dissatisfied	60 50 30 20 10
3. How much do you think stress affects your ability to maintain a healthy lifestyle?	a) Very little b) Somewhat c) A moderate amount d) Quite a bit e) An extreme amount	60 50 30 20 10

Question	Responses	Score
4. What is your current weight status?	a) I am maintaining a healthy weight.	60
	b) I am overweight but am losing weight, or underweight and gaining weight.	50
	c) I am overweight or underweight and I am maintaining this weight.	30
	d) I am overweight and I am gaining weight, or underweight and losing weight.	20
	e) I don't know.	10
5. What is your current smoking or tobacco use status?	a) I am tobacco free and have been for more than a year.	60
	b) I have been tobacco free for at least 6 months.	50
	c) I am in the process of quitting.	30
	d) I am planning to quit in the next 6 months.	20
	e) I use tobacco and have no intentions to quit.	10

Well-Being Score *(Add answers 1-5 in this section)* _____

TOTAL BLI SCORE _____

(Add Nutrition, Activity, Well-Being scores)

Scoring the Balanced Life Survey

When you finish answering the questions on the BLI, add the points for each section and for the total BLI, and then copy them here:

BLI Nutrition Score: _____

BLI Activity Score: _____

BLI Well-Being Score: _____

TOTAL BLI SCORE _____

15 questions total

Nutrition: 350 points *(5 questions)*

Activity: 350 points *(5 questions)*

Well-Being: 300 points; 180 points for well-being *(3 questions)*, 120 points for weight management and tobacco *(2 questions)*

Total possible: 1,000 points.

To determine what your current BLI score means, look at the following chart:

Total Score	Nutrition or Activity Score	Well-Being Score	Descriptive Category
900–1,000	315–350	270–300	Superb balance
800–899	280–314	240–269	Excellent balance
700–799	245–279	210–239	Good balance
600–699	210–244	180–209	Making progress
500–599	175–209	150–179	Keep it up
499 and below	174 and below	149 and below	Get ready for the benefits of balance

You also can see where you stand on each domain of the BLI (nutrition, activity, or well-being)

Ready, Set. . . .

In chapter 3, I asked you to list up to five reasons or goals for starting *Your Plan for a Balanced Life* and highlight the three most important. As we head toward more specific goal-setting in the next chapter, consider how your preliminary goals match the results of your BLI. Which area do you need to work on most? Do any specific areas stand out? Do your scores on the BLI match up well with your expectations, or are there some surprises?

Keep these ideas handy as you go to the next chapter.

Where Would You Like to Go?
Goal Setting

If you don't know where you're going—
you could end up anywhere!

—Old proverb

"What's my next challenge? I'm ready!" Linda approaches
everything—even her annual health evaluation—with verve. "Life's
an adventure," she often says, "and I plan to make the most of every
minute. So where do I need to go?" Your quest for better balance in
life is also an adventure. And the best part is that you get to choose
exactly where you wish to go and how to get there. You'll have clearly
defined goals to point you in the right direction and carefully selected
strategies and action steps to take you to your destination. You will
have goals that target your needs and strategies, and steps to take that
will work within the realities of your life.

Why Set Goals and Plan?

Planning can feel so tedious when you are all fired up and ready to start taking action. So why take time to assess your needs and make specific plans?

In working with thousands of people on changing personal practices, I have found that people stumble on small issues. It's pretty easy to identify the cosmic changes you desire, such as "eat better," "make more time for family," or "start regular planned activity," but unless you break these broad general goals into more specific goals and implement them with specific strategies, you will never get beyond the dream of taking action.

Now is the time to call on your imagination and creativity—the possibilities for strategies that can work for you are endless. In the previous chapter, the Balanced Life Index helped you assess your strengths and weaknesses, and you identified up to five general goals for your plan.

Now that you've done that, your goal setting will go quickly.

Expand Your Plan with Interactive Online Tools at StartMakingChoices.com

StartMakingChoices.com is a free online program that helps you incorporate physical activity, nutritious food, and personal time into your busy lifestyle. It's easy to register, get started, and use—and it can help you take your program for balance to the next level.

The program offers you a personalized action plan with these tools to help you achieve balance:

1. A weekly meal plan that you can customize with:
   - Quick snacks
   - Convenient dinners
   - Easy homemade meals
   - Restaurant offerings
   - A log to track your nutrition and calories

How to Create Goals and Strategies

How you select and define your goals and strategies can have a lot to do with how successfully you achieve them.

Every goal or strategy you select should satisfy these criteria:

Specific. Your goal or strategy describes a straightforward action or behavior that you wish to accomplish.

Measurable. How can you tell when you've reached the goal or carried out the strategy? What measurement indicates success? "Be more active" isn't measurable. "Begin the Balanced Walking Plan on June 1" is.

Attainable. You can also think of this quality as action-oriented. It's something you can do, not something that's so big or outside your capability that it's just a pipe dream. If you are in your mid-forties and have never swum competitively, "become next Olympic swimming champion" is unattainable, but "become a swimming champion in our local and regional Senior Games" or even "compete in local and regional meets" may be attainable dreams.

Realistic. The goal or strategy has to be something that fits your realities and is doable. A goal or strategy should not require skills, resources, money, or time you don't

2. A customized activity plan
   - Daily and weekly activities. For example, start with walking; add strength training.
   - Fits your busy schedule
   - Charts your progress every day with online tracker
   - Ties into your overall plan for a balanced life

3. The key elements of well-being, plus
   - Learn how others manage stress
   - Discover why rest is critical
   - Find out how emotions affect well-being

4. Interactive tools
   - Health calculators (Body Mass Index, appropriate daily calorie level)
   - Interactive MyPyramid
   - Balanced Life Index

5. Interaction when you are away
   - Free monthly e-mail newsletter

have and cannot acquire. For example, choosing swimming as your major activity may not be realistic if the nearest pool is an hour away.

Timely. The goal or strategy must have a time frame in which you aim to complete it. For example, "lose ten pounds" might never happen unless you give yourself an end date, such as "lose ten pounds in the next three months."

Goals, Strategies, and Action Steps

At the end of this chapter, you will find a sample goal-setting worksheet. You will also find easy-to-use on-line worksheets at StartMakingChoices.com. After you read through the following chapters on nutrition, activity, and well-being, you'll use this worksheet to form goals for each of these three areas—and develop strategies and action steps to achieve your goals.

You will:

1. Set a specific goal that addresses your general goal.
2. Identify specific strategies to implement this goal.
3. Identify specific action steps to accomplish each strategy.

If your BLI score was low in nutrition, for instance, one of your general goals may be to eat more fruits and vegetables. You can translate that into action using these three steps:

Goal:

Increase fruit intake to recommended three servings daily.

Strategies:

Eat at least one more serving of fruit daily during the work week. Keep stocked fruit bowl on the kitchen counter.

Action Steps:

▲ *Take fruit for my afternoon snack three days a week.*

▲ *Have fruit for dessert for two dinners a week.*

▲ *Reach for a piece of fruit from the bowl instead of another snack.*

▲ *Pack away less nutritious snacks so I won't be tempted by them.*

There is no limit to how many strategies and action steps you can brainstorm. Your objective at this first step in planning is to create as many ideas as you can. Think of it as your "pantry" where you have all the ingredients you need to put together an overall program and map out an actual program calendar.

You don't have to work on the worksheets and the following chapters in order. If your BLI scores indicate that you are okay in the nutrition department but need to add activity, you may want to skip ahead to the activity chapter and work on that first, and add nutrition later.

Whichever of the three chapters you start with, as you work through it, look for specific strategies, action steps, and tools you can use. Note ideas and tools you'd like to use on your goal-setting worksheets at the end of each chapter.

Your Plan for a Balanced Life
Goal-Setting Worksheet

Goal 1: _____

    Strategy: _____

        Action Steps: _____

    Strategy: _____

        Action Steps: _____

    Strategy: _____

        Action Steps: _____

Goal 2: _____

    Strategy: _____

        Action Steps: _____

    Strategy: _____

        Action Steps: _____

    Strategy: _____

        Action Steps: _____

Goal 3: _____

    Strategy: _____

        Action Steps: _____

    Strategy: _____

        Action Steps: _____

    Strategy: _____

        Action Steps: _____

Your Balanced Nutrition Plan

"Diet is 'die' with a T on the end!"

This exclamation spilled out of a potential reader when we asked what she desired in a plan for balanced nutrition. The sentiment is shared by millions of Americans who are tired of diets. Diets promise "amazing results in record time," but too often your reward for sticking with austere or bizarre eating plans is unbalanced nutrition and an introduction to yo-yo weight management. Nothing could be further from balance.

So here's a promise. You will not find the word "diet" used in connection with the Balanced Nutrition Plan. Whether you want to maintain a healthy weight or lose weight, reduce your potential risk factors for chronic disease, or eat to manage an existing health problem, you can adapt the Balanced Nutrition Plan to meet your needs. And you can use it to design meals to meet the nutritional needs for your family.

The Balanced Nutrition Plan relies on the MyPyramid Food Guidance System, which is based on the Dietary Guidelines for

Americans (DGA), research-based nutritional recommendations for people over two years of age.

A recent review found that the DGAs are consistent with nutrition practices recommended for many chronic diseases such as high blood pressure, cholesterol problems, or heart disease.[1] If you are managing such a condition, however, check with your physician before changing your eating or activity levels. (A person with diabetes, for instance, may need to have her insulin dosage reduced if she changes what she eats and becomes physically active.)

Enhancing the Pleasures of the Table

Many people think that food that's good for you doesn't taste good, but nutritious can be delicious—*should* be delicious. One of the joys of life is sharing a meal with those you love. Throughout history, breaking bread together and sharing hospitality have been a way to celebrate both daily connectedness and important occasions. Seeking balance in nutrition is about enjoying the pleasures of good food as much as it is about choosing food that's good for you. This chapter can help you achieve both.

Before I went to medical school, I trained as a chef in a French restaurant, and I remain an avid amateur chef. Preparing meals with my wife is important to us both as a way to do something together and to treat our family to tasty, nutritious meals.

Remember that all the facts, tips, techniques, and advice in this chapter are just tools to help you create the balance in good eating that you desire for yourself and your family. The choices are yours!

Balanced Nutrition and Why You Need It

The human body needs more than forty nutrients to support growth, normal functioning, and health.[2] These nutrients include both macronutrients (carbohydrates, fats, and proteins) that supply the body with "fuel" and micronutrients (vitamins, minerals, and other substances that have an effect on the body's tissues) that support the growth, maintenance, and health of many systems. Because no one food supplies all these nutrients, we must get them from the variety of foods and beverages we consume. Balanced nutrition is getting the right amount of all nutrients for health and weight management—neither too little nor too much.

Balanced nutrition is getting the right amount of all nutrients for health and weight management.

All food can fit into a healthful and balanced approach to daily nutrition, and consuming a variety of foods and beverages helps achieve balance. Getting your nutrients mostly from food, rather than supplements, is best because research suggests that the many substances in whole foods work together to enhance the effectiveness of many micronutrients, such as certain vitamins and antioxidants.

Here's a reminder of a few important perks of balanced nutrition:

▲ Supports normal functioning and health of the body's structures and systems.

▲ Supports development of strong bones, muscles, and other systems for growing children and adolescents, and maintenance of bones and muscles for adults.

▲ Helps you maintain a healthy weight.

▲ Helps protect you against chronic diseases such as heart disease, high blood pressure, diabetes, and some cancers.

▲ Enhances the pleasures of the table. With proper attention to balance, there's room for all foods in your nutrition plan.

How Balanced Is Your Nutrition Now?

Let's look at your score on the nutrition section of the BLI. If your total nutrition score is 250 or above, you're doing a good job. Usually, however, there's still room for improvement. If your nutrition score is below 250, it's time to start working on your daily nutrition habits.

What If You Don't Plan to Start With Nutrition?

Perhaps, based on your BLI scores, you've decided to start with activity. In that case, you could choose to jump to chapter 7, Your Balanced Activity Plan. But don't skip the section about the nutritional basics. Even if you don't create a nutrition plan right away, you may see smart nutritional modifications that you can easily start slipping into your daily routine for a head start on gradual change.

What Areas Need Work?

Take a look at the copy of the BLI where you circled your answers. Based on your answers, indicate whether you need to increase or decrease your intake of these foods and whether you need to gain, lose, or maintain your weight:

Fruit	*Increase*	*Decrease*	*Maintain*
Vegetables	*Increase*	*Decrease*	*Maintain*
Milk/equivalent	*Increase*	*Decrease*	*Maintain*
Whole-grain foods	*Increase*	*Decrease*	*Maintain*
Foods high in fat, sugar, and/or empty calories	*Increase*	*Decrease*	*Maintain*
Body weight	*Increase*	*Decrease*	*Maintain*

Keep your evaluation in mind as you read the following sections on essential foods for balanced nutrition.

Your Body Mass Index (BMI)

At this point, it's also a good idea to determine your Body Mass Index, known as BMI. The BMI takes into account both your height and weight and provides a reliable estimate of your weight status. Using the BMI chart on page 165, find your height on the left and then find the category closest to your current weight. Your BMI number is at the top of that column. What is your weight status based on your BMI?

Normal	Overweight	Obese
19-24.9	**25-29.9**	**30+**

You can also calculate your BMI online at StartMakingChoices.com. Click on "tools," then "health calculators." The calculator will give your BMI and your ideal calorie range based on your BMI and activity level.

Your Daily Energy Intake Level

Another helpful figure to know as you plan is your appropriate estimated daily energy intake—about how many calories you should be eating to maintain a healthy weight. You can get a general idea using the table on page 164, which was used for the MyPyramid Food

Intake Patterns. The MyPyramid Food Intake Patterns are data that MyPyramid uses to set recommendations of servings to meet daily calorie levels for individuals based on gender, age, and activity levels. Knowing the general recommended range for your age and activity level can help you set your goals for nutrition and activity.

Your Balanced Life Index (BLI)

The nutrient questions on the BLI represent key food groups where most Americans fall short—usually far short—of recommendations. It asks questions about weight status because 66 percent of adult Americans are either overweight or obese.

This questionnaire doesn't directly address some food groups: the meat and beans group (protein), refined grains, and oils. Most Americans consume more than adequate amounts of food from these groups.

The BLI is based on a 2,000 calorie diet. If your recommended intake is lower or higher, the BLI may not be as accurate for you. You may wish to take the BLI online, (www.StartMakingChoices.com), where the nutrition questions target individualized calorie levels.

Your Balanced Life Index score will give you a workable baseline to help select the changes or modifications you need in eating habits. But keeping a three-day food diary can give you the most accurate picture of your eating patterns. Some of us, for instance, are very surprised to see how many snacks we eat throughout the day. You'll find a blank food diary checklist on page 161. Use the results from your food diary to retake the BLI or to compare to the recommendations for each food group in the following pages.

Balancing Energy and Nutrition

Our bodies require energy to stay alive and to function properly. This energy comes from three macronutrients—carbohydrate, protein, and fat. And the body needs all three to survive (no, you can't leave fat out). Carbohydrate, protein, and fat are the only nutrients that provide calories or energy. (Alcohol provides calories but isn't considered a nutrient because it's not necessary for survival or health.)

The body also requires micronutrients, such as vitamins and minerals, for proper functioning, but these nutrients don't provide calories. To maintain all the body's functions, we need an appropriate balance of all micronutrients required for health. And our bodies also need water.

Our bodies require energy to stay alive and to function properly.

We need both balanced energy and balanced nutrients: Balanced energy means eating only the calories needed to maintain a healthy weight (neither gain nor lose weight); balanced nutrients means eating the right amount of nutrients to maintain health.

No matter what your weight, you need the right balance of energy and nutrients. If you want to lose weight, then you will need to reduce the calories you consume or increase those you burn (or both) while balancing foods to supply all the nutrients your body needs. If you want to gain weight, you need to take in more calories than you burn.

Fruits and Vegetables

Balanced nutrition goals based on MyPyramid are:

▲ *Eat at least 2 cups of fruit daily.* Examples of one cup: a large (8-inch) banana, a large peach, a medium mango, or a small apple. Examples of $\frac{1}{2}$ cup: a small orange, $\frac{1}{2}$ of a 4-inch grapefruit, $\frac{1}{2}$ cup of strawberries, or $\frac{1}{4}$ cup of raisins.

▲ *Eat at least 2$\frac{1}{2}$ cups of vegetables daily.* Examples of one cup: a large baked sweet potato or 2 cups of raw spinach. Examples of $\frac{1}{2}$ cup: $\frac{1}{2}$ cup of cooked green beans, cooked kidney beans, raw broccoli, cauliflower florets, or cooked leafy greens.

Fruits and vegetables are nutrient powerhouses, offering big nutritional bang for calories spent. Most fruits and vegetables are naturally low in fat and sodium and high in fiber, and they have no cholesterol (no plant-based food does). Large studies show that people who regularly eat plenty of fruits and vegetables as part of a healthy diet have a lower risk of many diseases, including heart disease, stroke, type 2 diabetes, and some cancers, particularly those of the digestive track.

Making Calories Count

Balancing calories is important, but what's in those calories is important too. Vegetables, fruits, whole grains, dairy foods and lean meats have a lot of nutrients relative to their calories making them nutrient dense.

Say you're choosing from two 500-calorie meals. One has roasted chicken, mashed potatoes, and steamed carrots. The other is a cold-cut sandwich with mayo and chips. Which is the more nutrient-dense meal? The chicken meal!

Get the most nutrition out of your calories; think nutrient density.

Nutrition Strengths of Fruits and Vegetables

Fruits and vegetables are important sources of minerals, vitamins, fiber, and phytochemicals.

Potassium is a mineral that helps to keep your blood pressure at healthy levels. Good sources of potassium include baked sweet potatoes and white potatoes; tomato puree, paste, and sauce (including canned varieties, such as Hunt's); green soybeans (the popular *edamame*) and other beans; bananas, cantaloupe and honeydew melons; orange juice, prunes and prune juice; carrot juice; dried apricots and peaches; and spinach.

Folate, also known as folic acid, is a B vitamin that helps the body produce red blood cells and is needed to help build DNA and RNA. Adequate intake of folate is particularly important for women who may become or are pregnant because it helps prevent neural tube defects and spina bifida while the baby is developing. Leafy green vegetables such as spinach and turnip greens are good sources of folate (the word "folate" comes from the Latin for "leaf"). Many breakfast cereals are also fortified with folic acid, and eating fruit with them is a great idea. Other good sources include broccoli, asparagus, avocados, black-eyed and green peas, oranges, and orange and tomato juice.

Vitamin C helps the body grow and repair its tissues, including helping cuts and wounds heal. It's a major antioxidant. Citrus fruit is, of course, a good source of vitamin C, as are red and green peppers, guava, strawberries, cantaloupe, Brussels sprouts, broccoli, snow pea pods, tomato juice, kale, fresh pineapple, and mango.

Fruits and vegetables are important sources of minerals, vitamins, fiber, and phytochemicals.

Dietary fiber is associated with lower blood cholesterol and lower risk of heart disease. Fiber may also help protect against some cancers. It also helps prevent constipation. Because fiber can't be digested, it contributes to the lower calorie content of many vegetables. Fiber is one of the reasons vegetables can help fill you up without too many calories. Good sources of fiber include many whole grains, dried beans, peas, and lentils; raspberries and blackberries; pears, prunes, spinach, turnip and collard greens, apples with skin, bananas, oranges, winter squash, broccoli, and okra.

Vitamin A helps regulate the immune system and protects against infection. Vitamin A is important to vision, bone growth, and cell division. It is present in animal and plant foods. Carotenoids, such as beta-carotene, are found in orange and leafy green vegetables and convert to vitamin A as needed. Meats and dairy foods are rich in vitamin A. Vitamin A in the form of beta-carotene is found in carrot juice and carrots, sweet potatoes, pumpkin, spinach, collards and other greens, winter squash, and cantaloupe.

Vitamin E is a powerful antioxidant that helps protect the body's cells from free radicals, the damaging byproducts that occur when the body burns food for energy. Vegetable sources of vitamin E include nuts and seeds, peanut butter, spinach, broccoli, turnip greens, canned tomato products (paste, puree, sauce), and vegetable oils such as sunflower, safflower, canola, corn, peanut, and olive oils. (More about vitamin E sources when we look at the meat and protein group and at oils.)

Phytochemicals are bioactive plant substances that are not nutrients but work with nutrients to help protect our cells and bodies against damage and disease. To date, more than one thousand have been found, and we're just beginning to understand the role these substances may play in human health. Many are related to plant pigments and are found in brightly colored fruit. Examples include flavanoids found in red, blue, and purple berries and grapes, isoflavones found in soy foods and other legumes, and polyphenols found in tea.

Getting the Most from Your Fruits and Vegetables

Here are a few strategies for getting the most value and enjoyment out of fruits and vegetables:

Preparation makes a difference. French-fried potatoes, baked potatoes stuffed with butter and sour cream, and vegetables topped with cream or cheese sauce may taste good, but eating them too often will throw your fat intake and energy intake out of balance. Instead, make baked "fries" in the oven with regular or sweet potatoes. Make a stir-fry with plenty of veggies. Steam your side veggies lightly and sprinkle a small amount of grated cheese on top. Experiment!

Go for variety and color. Different fruits and vegetables contain different nutrients. Eating a variety of fruits and vegetables ensures that you get a broad range of necessary nutrients. Many of the nutrients are associated with color; choosing a variety of colors when you select fruits and vegetables can mean receiving a wider range of nutrients.

Select fruit and vegetables in season for flavor and economy. Produce is best when it is in season, and the cost is usually lower. Check out local farmer's markets. Community Supported Agriculture groups (CSAs) support a farmer, who provides the group with fresh fruits and vegetables and often other products such as eggs. Local supermarkets also have a wide selection of fresh vegetables and fruits in season. Out of season, frozen, or canned fruits and vegetables may be of better quality than fresh fruits and vegetables that have been shipped in from a continent away. In prepared foods look for items that include vegetables, such as Healthy Choice meals.

Whole Grains

Balanced nutrition goals based on MyPyramid are:
▲ *Make at least half of my grain-based foods whole grain.*
▲ *Eat at least three whole-grain daily ounce equivalents.*

Bread has been called "the staff of life" for millennia because cereal grains have formed the basic foodstuff in many cultures from prehistoric times. The most common grains are wheat, rice, oats, corn, barley, and rye. In addition to bread, grain-based foods include pasta (noodles), hot and cold breakfast cereals, flatbreads (tortillas, chapatis, and pita), crackers, grits, or polenta.

Eating a variety of fruits and vegetables ensures that you get a broad range of necessary nutrients.

Grain-based foods are made from either whole grains or refined grains. Whole-grain foods contain the whole kernel of the grain—the bran (outer layer), germ (plant embryo), and endosperm (germ's food supply)—including all its naturally occurring nutrients. Refined grains have had most of the bran and germ removed by milling. Refining makes the grain more shelf-stable but less nutritious because the bran and germ contain most of the fiber, B vitamins, and iron found in whole grains. To make up for this loss, many refined grains are enriched by adding B vitamins and iron, but the fiber and other nutrients are not added.

Whole Grains vs. Refined Grains

Whole Grains	Refined Grains
Whole-wheat flour	White flour
Oats and oatmeal	N/A (all oat foods are whole grain)
Brown rice	White rice
Cracked wheat (bulgar)	Couscous, cream of wheat
Whole cornmeal	Degermed cornmeal
Whole-rye flour	Refined rye flour
Popcorn	N/A
Buckwheat	N/A
Barley	N/A

Nutrition Strengths of Whole Grains

Many whole grains are a good source of fiber, which is associated with a reduced risk of heart disease. Whole grains also provide B vitamins, minerals, antioxidants, and phytonutrients. B vitamins such as thiamin, riboflavin, and niacin help the body get energy from carbohydrates, fat, and protein. Folate, as mentioned earlier, helps in the formation of red blood cells. The B vitamins also help keep the nervous system healthy. Antioxidants and other phytonutrients complement the function of micronutrients.

Most whole grains provide magnesium, selenium, and iron. Magnesium helps bone development and has a structural role in cell membranes and chromosomes. Magnesium also plays a role in over three hundred metabolic processes, such as helping the muscles release energy. Selenium is a trace element that the body needs in small amounts to help protect cells from oxidation and to support the immune system. Iron helps protect against anemia; whole grains are a non-animal source of iron. Iron absorption is increased if foods with vitamin C are consumed at the same time.

Eating a healthy diet rich in whole grains may help in weight management. Eating at least three servings (ounce equivalents) daily of whole grains has been associated with a lower risk of heart disease, stroke, type 2 diabetes, and some cancers.

Tapping the Nutrition of Whole Grains

These strategies may help you go for the whole grains:

Availability. Demand for whole grains has been growing, but whole-grain products constitute only 10 to15 percent of the grain-based foods on market shelves. Some of the available whole-grain foods include oatmeal, kasha, whole-grain ready-to-eat cereals, whole-wheat breads, whole-wheat muffins, and whole-wheat bagels, popcorn, whole-wheat and buckwheat pasta, whole corn grits (speckled heart grits), and grains such as barley, brown rice, wild rice, quinoa, and millet. Add a little barley to your homemade vegetable soup, or serve your favorite marinara sauce atop buckwheat pasta. For a whole-grain snack, try microwave popcorn, such as Orville Redenbacher's Smart Pop.

Eating a healthy diet rich in whole grains may help in weight management.

Identifying. Don't rely on brown color or a label that says "multigrain" or "wheat bread." If the item is labeled "100 percent whole wheat," then all of the wheat used in the product must be whole grain. For other items, look at the ingredients list on the package label. If the first listed ingredient has "whole" in front of it, such as whole-wheat flour, the product is likely to be mostly whole grain. The Whole Grains Council has even created a packaging symbol shaped like a stamp that will indicate the number of grams of whole grains in the product.

What about products labeled "white whole wheat"? Most wheat grown in the U.S. is hard red wheat. However, hard white wheat is also grown in North America. The outer bran of white wheat is lighter in color, making lighter whole-wheat flour that also has a milder taste that many people may prefer. Research suggests that the whole-grain nutrient value of red and white whole wheat is similar.

Gluten-free whole grains. People with celiac disease or gluten sensitivity cannot eat wheat (including durum, spelt, Kamut®, einkorn, and emmer), rye, triticale, oats, or barley. Buckwheat, corn, millet, quinoa, and rice have no gluten.

Milk, Milk Products, and Milk Equivalents

Balanced nutrition goal based on MyPyramid is:
▲ *Consume three cups of fat-free or low-fat milk, milk products, or milk equivalents daily.*

Nutritional Strengths of Milk, Milk Products, and Milk Equivalents

For most Americans, milk and milk products are our chief sources of calcium, which is critical for developing bone mass, preserving bone health, and preventing osteoporosis. Milk products are often fortified with vitamin D, which helps in calcium absorption and maintaining proper calcium levels. One cup of plain yogurt has 452 mg of calcium (150 calories), one cup of fat-free milk has 300 mg calcium (83 calories), and 1.5 ounces of Swiss cheese has 335 mg calcium (160 calories), for example. Dairy products such as fat-free milk, yogurt, and buttermilk are good sources of potassium, which helps maintain healthy blood pressure. Milk products also are a good source of protein. When consumed in fat-free or low-fat forms, milk contributes little or no saturated fat. Caution: Butter, cream, and cream cheese are not included in the milk food group because they have no calcium and may be high in fat.

Calcium is critical for bone mass development, bone health, and preventing osteoporosis.

Tapping the Nutrition of Milk Products

Go fat-free or low-fat. Most popular milk products come in fat-free or low-fat versions. These have all the nutritional power of whole milk products without the saturated fat and extra calories. Even some hard cheeses have low-fat versions.

Choose a variety of milk products. You can make milk products a vital part of your meal planning without having to drink three glasses a day. Yogurt with fruit makes a great lunch or snack. Use cottage cheese and ricotta in lasagna and other dishes. Enjoy a fruit smoothie made with fat-free milk or yogurt. Have some hot chocolate or low-fat ice cream for a treat.

Include cheese. Many cheeses that are high in fat are also high in flavor. A little bit of hard grating cheese such as parmesan or Romano can jazz up a whole dish. There's room for all cheeses in your balanced nutrition plan if you allow for their fat content in your overall plan.

Milk Modifications

▲ Ask for fat-free milk in your latte or cappuccino.

▲ Low-fat plain yogurt is a great baked potato topper. Add chives for extra flavor.

▲ Try low-fat yogurt or fat-free sour cream instead of regular sour cream in your favorite dip recipes.

▲ When a recipe calls for cream and you're watching your calorie and fat intake, try using nonfat half-and-half or evaporated skim milk.

▲ Make your cream soups or hot cereals with fat-free milk.

What about lactose intolerance? Lactose-free and lower-lactose products work for some people. Milk, yogurt, and cheese come in these forms. If you eat few or no milk products, explore other sources of calcium such as calcium-fortified soy beverages and fruit juice. Also leafy green vegetables and soybeans are good sources of calcium, but the calcium content is lower and typically less absorbable.

Does ice cream count? Frozen milk treats contain small amounts of calcium and vitamin A. Choose low-fat ice cream or low-fat frozen yogurt, and keep portions small. I know a young woman who successfully lost almost a hundred pounds, and her meal plan included low-fat ice cream or frozen yogurt three or four nights a week. She bought her single scoop at the nearby ice cream shop, so no temptation resided in the freezer.

Explore other calcium sources. Nondairy sources of calcium that are readily absorbed by the body include canned sardines and salmon (bones included), calcium-set tofu (bean curd), and fortified beverages. Your body's ability to use calcium in these foods varies.

Proteins—Meat, Fish, Eggs, Beans, and Nuts

Balanced nutrition goals based on MyPyramid are:
▲ *Eat five to six ounce equivalents of protein-rich foods daily.*
▲ *If selecting meat, poultry or fish, remember that amount is about two three-ounce portions.*

You can call this group "protein potpourri" because it contains so many different foods. Meat, poultry, fish, eggs (or Egg Beaters), beans and peas, nuts and seeds are all included. Their nutritional profiles differ, too. Some cuts of meat are higher in saturated fat, while fish and the plant-based proteins such as beans, nuts, and seeds have more healthful monounsaturated and polyunsaturated fats. Animal proteins contain cholesterol; plant-based proteins do not. So you need to select your protein sources for balance.

What Do We Get from These Foods?

In addition to protein, these foods supply B vitamins, vitamin E, iron, zinc, and magnesium. Proteins are the building blocks for many parts and systems of the body, such as muscles, bones, cartilage, skin, blood, enzymes, hormones, and vitamins.

Meats such as beef and pork, for instance, are typically higher in saturated fat than fish or nut sources. Because eating too much saturated fat can increase the risk of heart disease, our goal should be to limit the amount of saturated fat we consume. On the other hand, eating foods rich in polyunsaturated and monounsaturated fats lowers the risk of heart disease. Eating fish rich in polyunsaturates called omega-3 fatty acids, for example, appears to promote

Eating a variety of foods enables you to get sufficient protein and varied nutrients.

cardiovascular health. Fish rich in polyunsaturates include salmon, trout, and herring. Again, the message is balance.

Nuts and seeds are a good source of vitamin E, a powerful antioxidant that helps protect the body's cells from oxidation damage. Large population studies have shown that people who regularly eat nuts and seeds in moderate amounts have a 30 to 50 percent lower risk of heart attack or cardiovascular disease.[3]

Tapping the Nutrition of Proteins

Eat a variety of foods from the protein group. All foods with protein aren't alike. They have differing levels of fat, for instance. Also some proteins, typically those from animal foods, have a complete set of the amino acids the body uses to build new protein, and others, typically those from plant foods, have an incomplete set. Eating a variety of foods enables you to get sufficient protein and the varied nutrients available in this food group.

Select lean protein. If you eat beef, pork, or lamb, select lean cuts and trim visible fat. When you select chicken, remove the skin, which is where most of the fat and cholesterol resides, before cooking or eating. Roasting a chicken with the skin on, for instance, doesn't add fat to the meat and may help keep it moist during cooking; just remove the skin before you eat it. Some prepared foods, such as Healthy Choice products, include leaner meats.

Enjoy fish. Research suggests that eating fish twice a week can help you take advantage of omega-3 fatty acids. Fish such as salmon, trout, and herring are rich in omega-3s.

Balance your plant proteins. Plant foods are low in certain essential amino acids, unlike meat and fish. (Meat and fish are complete protein sources alone.) The great thing is that the amino acids in one plant food can make up for whatever amino acids are low in the other food. Especially if you are a vegetarian, combine foods over the course of the day such as beans and lentils with other foods such as bread or rice to create a complete protein. For instance, if you eat a legume (bean, lentil, split pea, etc.) also eat a grain (wheat, rye, barley, etc.).

A hearty bean soup with whole-grain cornbread is a real family pleaser on a cold winter night. In the summer, a cold lentil salad made with tomatoes, basil, and green onions and served with crackers can hit the spot. Don't forget "old reliable", the peanut butter sandwich; put it on whole-grain bread and please the kids or the kid in you.

Oils—and Other Fats

Balanced nutrition goals based on MyPyramid are:
▲ *Select healthy oils to keep fat intake between 20 and 35 percent of daily calories.*
▲ *Keep my choice of foods with saturated fat low and avoid trans fats whenever possible.*

We have heard the message that we should decrease our fat intake. Unfortunately, that message also seems to have translated to "fat is bad." Actually, fat is good—if it's the right fat and in the right quantity. Our bodies need fat to function just as they need carbohydrates and protein. The healthiest fats are polyunsaturated and monounsaturated fats; they contain the essential fatty acids our bodies need. These fats typically come in the form of oil and are liquid at room temperature.

Saturated fats are solid at room temperature. Consuming saturated fat in excess is linked to elevated LDL cholesterol, which increases the risk of heart disease. Butter and the fat in beef and other meats is saturated fat. So-called tropical plant oils (coconut oil, palm kernel oil) are also high in saturated fat. When liquid oils are hydrogenated to make them solid, they become "trans fats," a type of saturated fat that appears to significantly increase cholesterol. Some, but not all, stick margarines and solid vegetable shortening are examples of trans fats that may be found in your kitchen. In commercial baked goods and other processed foods, trans fats will be declared on the label. Many food companies are either reducing or removing trans fats from their products.

Our goal is to balance our intake of fats so that we consume healthy amounts of oils and only small amounts of solid fats.

Our goal is to balance our intake of fats so that we consume healthy amounts of oils and only small amounts of solid fats.

Nutritional Strengths and Drawbacks of Oil and Solid Fat

Fats supply energy and essential fatty acids to the body and serve as a carrier for important fat-soluble vitamins such as vitamins A, D, E, and K. Fat is part of the membrane of every cell, so we need fats in the form of healthy oils.

Oils from vegetable sources and nut sources contain primarily monounsaturated and polyunsaturated fats that do not raise our LDL cholesterol (a risk for heart disease). Common vegetable oils include canola, corn, cottonseed, olive, peanut, safflower, soybean, and sunflower oils. Oils high in monounsaturated fat can play a role in maintaining HDL cholesterol, the "good" type that helps protect the cardiovascular system by transporting cholesterol away from artery walls. Oils high in monounsaturates include olive oil, canola oil, and avocado oil; nuts are also high in monounsaturates.

Saturated fat and trans fat both raise LDL cholesterol, the "bad" type associated with higher risk of cardiovascular disease. High levels of trans fats appear to give a one-two punch for risk: They raise "bad" LDL cholesterol and lower "good" HDL cholesterol. Most of the trans fats we eat come from manufactured food products. Read food labels for amounts of trans fats.

Tapping the Nutrition of Healthy Oils

Go lean. For many of us, a steak on the grill, a succulent chop, or a slice of smoky ham are among the greatest pleasures of eating. These selections can fit in your balanced plan if you think moderation and lean. Moderation means not every day, and lean means select lean cuts, trim visible fat, and grill instead of fry.

Enjoy nuts and seeds. Sprinkling chopped nuts over a salad or your cereal, having a sunflower seed snack, or featuring avocadoes in a sandwich can be delicious ways to tap the benefits of unsaturated oils.

Enjoy fried foods in moderation. Even when fried in vegetable oil, fried foods absorb oil. The smart choice here is simply to choose these foods less frequently and, when you do, pair them with lower-fat foods to stay in balance.

Discretionary Calories

A "discretionary calorie" is MyPyramid's way of referring to the calories left over after you have eaten foods that provide the vitamins, minerals, and other nutrients your body needs each day. If you approach your daily nutrition needs in a balanced way, you may occasionally have calories left over and can choose some foods to eat just because you enjoy them. You can choose them "at your discretion."

These calories can come from any food group. You may wish to use them for foods that have added sugar or higher fat content, for example. MyPyramid treats alcohol as discretionary calories.

Most people have only a limited number of discretionary calories—about one hundred to three hundred for most. If you don't get much physical activity, you may have even fewer. You can maximize your discretionary calories in two ways. First, you can select foods that give you more nutrients for the calories consumed. For example, fruits and vegetables provide more nutrients for fewer calories than foods that are high in fat or sugar. Lean cuts of meat such as eye-of-round beef roast or pork tenderloin provide similar protein for fewer calories than fattier cuts such a beef chuck roast or pork shoulder. Second, you can increase the amount of regular activity you get. People who are more active burn more calories. More activity also builds lean muscle mass and boosts metabolism, which further increases the number of calories the body burns.

Here are some ways that you can make the most of your discretionary calories:

▲ **Choose smaller portions.** Buy candy in bite-sized portions and eat just one or two. Select cookies, cakes, and other sweet treats in calorie-controlled portions. Dip one scoop of ice cream rather than two. Share a restaurant entrée with a friend.

Savory Salt Savers

Keeping your salt intake under 2,300 mg (about one teaspoon) daily can help maintain healthy blood pressure. To reduce salt:

▲ use chopped fresh herbs, lemon juice, or lemon zest to season foods.

▲ use low-sodium broth when cooking.

▲ don't add salt to steaming or cooking water for vegetables; sprinkling a little salt directly on the vegetables when they are ready to serve adds flavor with much less sodium.

▲ **Use a small amount** of chocolate sauce or fruit syrup over a baked pear or apple. Grate a small portion of parmesan, Romano, or sharp cheddar cheese over veggies, pasta, or potatoes. One slice of salami in a lean turkey sandwich makes a big difference in taste with only a small number of calories.

▲ V**ary your choices.** Choosing to spend your discretionary calories from day to day can enhance satisfaction and your sense of balance and freedom.

The Value of Water

The S.O.S. Where's Dinner Planner

At times in every family nothing goes according to schedule—or you are just flat out of ideas for meals. Here's a sanity saver. Sit down with our weekly meal planner on page 181 and use it as a template to create menus that everyone likes. Be sure to keep the ingredients on hand. You can vary it by including dishes that you don't ordinarily think of but that you like and that are quick to fix. Include some that other family members can make. Tape it to the back of a cupboard or pantry door. Then when desperation hits, look at the meal plan and choose a meal that works. Keep a shopping list handy to replace missing ingredients.

One of the ways you can jump-start your goal to better balance is to drink plenty of water. Water makes up more than half of our bodies—about 60 percent for men and 55 percent for women. Water plays a role in every biochemical reaction in our bodies. In addition to water in the solid food we eat women need about nine cups of fluid a day and men thirteen cups to replace what we use in the day's ordinary activities.[4] Although we get about 20 percent of the fluid we need from the foods we eat, we need to drink fluids to provide that other 80 percent. If you are dehydrated, drinking water throughout the day makes you alert and helps allay fatigue.

Any beverage you drink will contribute water. Maintain balance in your choices by choosing appropriate servings of beverages that provide needed nutrients, such as milk and 100 percent fruit juice, along with plain water. Other beverages such as coffee and tea can also help meet your water needs.

Tracking Your Progress Toward Balance

Keeping track of your progress motivates you to keep going. For a quick check, retake the BLI weekly or every other week just before you plan your weekly menu. Give yourself credit for steps accomplished, even if they seem small. If you failed to follow any steps you set, think about why. Were you unrealistic about the preparation time or its fit in the family schedule? Try again or pick a new action step.

START MAKING CHOICES.com

If you've signed up online at StartMakingChoices.com, it's easy to log your daily meals, and the program will keep track of your progress day-to-day.

Also consider keeping a journal. It doesn't have to be fancy or formal. You could keep a journal online or in a spiral notebook. Use it to keep track of your progress and to write down ideas or evaluations that will help you keep going forward.

However you choose to track your progress, remember that progress—going forward—is your goal. When you evaluate how you are doing, always look for insights and ideas that can keep you moving forward.

Staying Balanced When Eating Out

Enjoying a meal out is one of life's pleasures. Often it's a busy schedule's answer to "When are we going to eat?" Business travel also keeps us dining out. Eating in a balanced way is not too hard to achieve, even if you travel thousands of miles a month.

Pick a restaurant that fits your goals. If given a choice between a buffet and a traditional restaurant, choose the restaurant. Select a lean protein, a salad, and a vegetable side, ask for whole-grain bread, and you're set. At lunch, a deli can be a great choice because you can select lean turkey, roast beef, or ham and have them build the sandwich just as you like. Choose tuna and chicken salads less often.

Celebratory occasions deserve special meals. There are times to just enjoy.

Make healthier fast-food choices. Most fast-food emporiums have some healthier choices these days. For breakfast, choose an English muffin sandwich (hold the cheese and sausage) or a bagel with peanut butter (or low-fat cream cheese), orange juice, and coffee. Lunch can be salad with dressing on the side or a small burger or chili with side salad or baked potato. If you can choose whole-grain pizza crust, go for it—ask for lots of veggies in the topping and half the normal amount of cheese.

Preparation makes the difference. Choose leaner entrees (chicken, fish, or lean beef) cooked in ways that don't add many extra calories from fat or rich sauces. Choose grilled over fried; vegetable-based or lighter sauces instead of cheese or alfredo.

Watch portion sizes. One of the biggest problems with dining out is that restaurant portions are large. You can order an appetizer as a main dish, split your meal with a friend, or divide the meal in half as soon as you get it and take the rest home for another meal. And some restaurants specialize in "small plate" menu items.

Go ahead and splurge sometimes. Celebratory occasions deserve special meals. There are times to just enjoy. Maybe your favorite food is higher in fat than you'd pick on an average day, but special occasions aren't average, are they? Just enjoy yourself. Don't feel guilty.

Holidays and Special Occasions

Good food and special recipes are integral parts of celebrations and parties. Just maintain balance. Enjoy modest servings. If you are going to a holiday meal or party in the evening, select leaner, lighter foods for breakfast and lunch that day. Go easy on the spirits and drink plenty of water. Pace yourself. Remember that you are in charge of what and how much you choose to eat. You can enjoy holiday meals and still feel good enough to get up the next morning and take your daily walk. Continuing your activity will help you enjoy holidays and celebrations.

Remember that you are in charge of what and how much you choose to eat.

Making It Real: How One Woman Personalized Her Family's Balanced Nutrition Plan

Martha, 37, has three young children aged 3, 6, and 8. She had gradually gained twenty-five pounds during her pregnancies that she never completely lost. Her nutritional habits had become a matter of convenience rather than a matter of conscientious choice. Martha knew it was time for a change.

When Martha took the survey, she scored 150 out of 350 in the nutrition section. She was eating less than half a cup of fruits and vegetables a day. While she consumed an average of one cup of milk a day, she chose whole milk over fat-free milk. She often cooked pasta for her family, and she tried to emphasize whole grains—she consumed about two ounces every day. Martha knew it was important to limit her intake of sweets, but she ate three servings daily, including a sweetened beverage and dessert after dinner.

Martha's score of 150 put her in the "get ready for the benefits of a more balanced lifestyle" category in nutrition. She was determined to take small steps to improve her nutritional balance. Martha chose one balanced nutrition practice to add each week for five weeks. During the first week, she bought fresh fruits and left them in a bowl on the table so she and her family could reach for fruit as a first choice for a snack. On the second week, she started increasing her vegetable intake. She included a salad and vegetable in every dinner she prepared.

In the third week Martha began using low-fat milk on her breakfast cereal. In the fourth week, she concentrated on purchasing whole-grain products, particularly whole-grain pasta and bagels. Finally, in week five, she made a concerted effort to eat sweets only for an occasional special treat. She substituted water or vegetable juice for her afternoon soda breaks.

Seeking balance means making gradual changes to arrive at a healthful approach to eating that you can sustain for a lifetime.

After five weeks, these changes had increased her nutrition score on the Balanced Life Index from 150 to 270, putting her firmly into the "good" category. She raised her total BLI score to 640 from its previous level of 520. At the end of the five weeks, Martha's daily nutrition was more balanced, and she felt confident that additional small changes would enable her to reach all her goals.

Personalizing Your Balanced Nutrition Plan

Before you write down the actual steps you can take to achieve better nutrition, remember three very important aspects of balance:
▲ Balance in nutrition is about eating well and pleasurably while including all the nutrients you need for health and well-being.

▲ Balance in nutrition is a long-term goal. Seeking balance means making gradual changes to arrive at a healthful approach to eating that you can sustain for a lifetime.

▲ Balance in nutrition is about reality—your reality. If you don't choose strategies and a pace that fit within the realities of your life, then you are setting yourself up for frustration and disappointment. If you choose well, you can happily achieve the changes you desire.

You can choose to work on one action step each week, until it has become habit, and the next week add the next action step.

If you feel your entire nutritional life needs revamping, and you're the type of person who likes to make a lot of changes at once, you can make a jumpstart by following the two-week meal plan on page 166. At the end of the two weeks, you can design your own meal plans (or repeat the two-week one) or sign up for an individualized weekly meal plan at StartMakingChoices.com. Registration is free, and after you've filled in your personal information, every week the program provides a new menu tailored to your needs. Don't like the recommended plan? You can customize it to fit your individual taste profile. The site offers nutritious receipes, plus you'll get a variety of tasty snack ideas. As you log the meals you've eaten, you'll be able to track how well you are managing your plan. The site's blogs will give you both expert and consumer perspectives on nutrition.

START
M︎AKING
CHOICES.com

YOUR PLAN: Balanced Nutrition Plan

Using the goal-setting worksheet at the end of this chapter, write down three specific nutrition goals, in order of priority. These may be something like:

1. Drink more water.

2. Reduce the number of fast-food meals.

3. Eat a healthy breakfast.

For each of these, come up with three strategies or action steps. Example:

1. Drink more water.

Strategy 1: Carry a bottle of water to work every day.

Strategy 2: Carry a bottle of water in the car.

Strategy 3: Drink water with lunch and dinner.

2. Reduce the number of fast-food meals.

Strategy 1: Keep healthy snacks in the car.

Strategy 2: Pack tasty lunches to take to work.

Strategy 3: Keep a batch of frozen homemade stew in the freezer for meals when you are too busy to cook.

3. Eat a healthy breakfast.

Strategy 1: Buy some breakfast foods on your grocery shopping trip.

Strategy 2: Get up ten minutes earlier.

Strategy 3: Know ahead of time what you are going to eat for breakfast.

Your Plan for a Balanced Life
Goal-Setting Worksheet: Nutrition

Goal 1: _____

    Strategy: _____

        Action Steps: _____

    Strategy: _____

        Action Steps: _____

    Strategy: _____

        Action Steps: _____

Goal 2: _____

    Strategy: _____

        Action Steps: _____

    Strategy: _____

        Action Steps: _____

    Strategy: _____

        Action Steps: _____

Goal 3: _____

    Strategy: _____

        Action Steps: _____

    Strategy: _____

        Action Steps: _____

    Strategy: _____

        Action Steps: _____

Your Balanced Activity Plan

Our bodies are meant to be in motion. An active life is a healthy life. Yet activity is often a neglected component of a balanced and healthy lifestyle.

In medicine, we often say that there are no magic bullets for improving health or preventing and curing disease. Activity, however, comes closest to being that "magic bullet." A fellow physician once said that if activity were a pill, it would be the most powerful and important medication ever developed!

We know that as people become more physically active, they feel better about themselves and derive many health benefits, including lower risk of heart disease, high blood pressure, diabetes, and cancer, and an ability to manage weight. Physically active people generally have less depression, are happier, and just seem to get more out of life.

My passion for physical activity springs not only from experiencing its many benefits in my own life but also from observing its life-changing impact on patients and research study participant. One of the first positions I held as a cardiologist at the University of

Massachusetts Medical School was director of the Cardiac Rehabilitation Program. In this capacity I saw the many physical and emotional benefits that patients recovering from heart attacks gained from their walking programs. My research team at Rippe Lifestyle Institute did a series of studies about walking that provided solid scientific evidence of the many benefits of walking.

Most people know that they should get more regular activity, but many are frustrated by trying to do it. This chapter will help you find ways you can become more active.

What Is Balanced Activity?

We want to live fully every day, functioning at our best physically and mentally. We want to be able to safely and energetically do all the tasks and activities of life—not just today but through all stages of our lives. The ability to function well requires cardiovascular fitness, strong muscles, flexibility, mobility, balance, and coordination.

The ability to function well requires cardiovascular fitness, strong muscles, flexibility, mobility, balance, and coordination.

Your Balanced Activity Plan includes programs for several types of activity that you can use to acquire health and fitness: aerobic activity, strength training, and flexibility training. We'll also look at choices for leisure time and recreational activities.

Let's look at the integrated components of our Balanced Activity Pyramid, based on recommendations from the Centers for Disease Control and the American College of Sports Medicine.

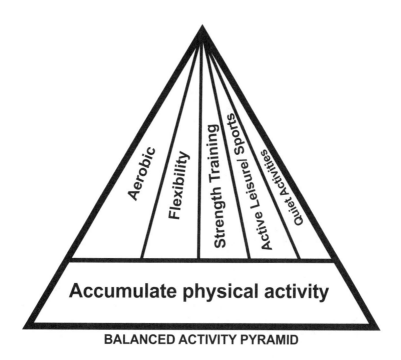

Aerobic

Flexibility

Strength Training

Active Leisure/ Sports

Quiet Activities

Accumulate physical activity

BALANCED ACTIVITY PYRAMID

A base of regular daily activity. Being active begins with accumulating moderate activity throughout your day. The core goal is to accumulate thirty minutes or more of moderate-intensity activity on most days of the week. Being more active throughout the day provides a great foundation for building all-around fitness with additional planned activities.

Aerobic activity. Aerobic activity, also called cardio activity, involves the repetitive use of the large muscles in the body to increase the heart rate and the consumption of oxygen (that's why it's called aerobic—literally meaning "in the presence of air"). By increasing the fitness of many body systems, aerobic activity helps protect against disease. Our Balanced Walking Plan lets you accumulate regular activity and build aerobic fitness. And it's easy for everyone to begin: It starts with a ten-minute walk.

Strength training. Strength training, also known as resistance exercise, lets you build strong muscles and lean muscle mass.

What Regular Activity Can Do for You

Here are some of the many benefits you can claim when you stay active. Regular activity:

▲ Enhances cardiovascular fitness.

▲ Keeps muscles, bones, and joints well-conditioned, strong, and able to perform well.

▲ Boosts physical energy and endurance.

▲ Helps maintain and build lean muscle mass, which boosts metabolism and helps you better manage weight.

▲ Reduces your risk of developing many chronic diseases, including heart disease, stroke, high blood pressure, lipid (cholesterol) disorders, type 2 diabetes, and certain cancers, and helps you manage many of these same conditions if you have them.

▲ Enhances mood and helps to prevent anxiety and depression.

▲ Helps manage and relieve stress.

▲ May help to preserve cognitive function as we age.

▲ Enhances physical appearance.

Typical strength-training exercises include weightlifting and calisthenics, and may be performed at home or at a gym. Because lean muscle tissue is the body's metabolic engine, strength training helps you manage your weight. Strong muscles also contribute to balance and your ability to do activities such as carrying the groceries, shifting boxes in the attic, or hauling that old chair off to the furniture bank. Strong muscles also help you keep up with the kids and grandkids.

Flexibility. Staying flexible is very important for maintaining functional fitness and range of motion for all parts of your body; it helps prevent injuries and falls because it improves balance. Flexibility exercises are also a good way to warm up before an aerobic or strength session and cool down afterwards. And the time spent doing flexibility exercises can enhance mind-body connections and relieve stress.

Active leisure and sports. Recreational activities have a smaller wedge on the Balanced Activity Pyramid because their primary purpose is not building physical fitness. However, most recreational activities are social; they connect you to others and yield benefits for emotional well-being. From tennis to family picnics, to softball, hiking, and canoeing, the enjoyment of active recreation can contribute to an overall balanced approach to activity.

Physical activity can be accumulated over the course of the entire day.

Quiet activities. Quiet activities get the thinnest wedge on the Pyramid, a little like the oils among the food groups for MyPyramid. But just as healthy oils are good for you in the right amounts, so are quieter, more sedentary activities such as watching TV, playing computer games, or playing Scrabble or cards. These quiet activities can also contribute to well-being—as long as they aren't your only activities.

How Much Activity You Need

A panel for the Centers for Disease Control and the American College of Sports Medicine, which I served on, studied the scientific literature in this area and issued one basic recommendation that has since been widely adopted by many health organizations:

Every U.S. adult should accumulate thirty minutes or more of moderate-intensity physical activity on most, preferably all, days of the week.[1]

There are two key words in this recommendation: *accumulate* and *moderate*. Physical activity can be accumulated over the course of the entire day, in time periods as little as ten minutes, as long as the accumulated amount of activity is thirty minutes or more. Moderate is an intensity level between light and intense. This means doing activities that require more than just casual activity but less than activities that would make you out of breath. Brisk walking is a classic example of moderate activity, a casual stroll at the mall would be considered light, and race walking would be considered intense exertion.

So the bottom line is that your basic goal should be to accumulate thirty minutes or more on most days at a moderate intensity. Larger goals for optimal fitness, strength, and flexibility will require additional activities, as discussed later in the chapter.

Fitting More Activity in Your Life

You may be thinking, "How can I fit in more activity with all the other demands I'm facing?" We all live under time pressures.

But if you look into the nooks and crannies of your life, you can find small ways to accumulate and increase activity, and before you know it, you will have your thirty minutes on most days. Here are some practical ways to incorporate more activity into your daily life. These are often called "incidental activities."

Around the House and Garden
▲ Chopping wood
▲ Cleaning bath and kitchen
▲ Cleaning garage or attic
▲ Cleaning gutters
▲ Cleaning windows
▲ Dusting
▲ Gardening, digging, planting, weeding
▲ Hanging pictures
▲ Mopping
▲ Mowing
▲ Picking up trash
▲ Playing with children or grandchildren
▲ Playing with pets
▲ Painting inside or outside your house
▲ Raking

▲ Redecorating

▲ Repairing; doing odd jobs

▲ Scrubbing

▲ Shoveling snow

▲ Standing while on the telephone; walking around while on a portable or cell phone

▲ Sweeping floors and walks

▲ Vacationing where you can be active

▲ Vacuuming

▲ Walking the dog

▲ Walking or biking to visit a neighbor (rather than driving)

▲ Walking to school

▲ Washing and waxing the car

▲ Woodworking; building shelves

On the Way to and at Work

▲ Brief stretching or calisthenics for break

▲ Biking to work

▲ Getting off bus or train a stop or two early and walking the rest of the way

▲ Parking in the side of the lot farthest from your office

▲ Standing while on the telephone and perhaps doing some toe raises

▲ Using the stairs rather than the elevator

▲ Walking down the hall occasionally to speak to a coworker rather than using e-mail or the phone

▲ Walking to work and/or lunch

▲ Walking ten minutes during lunch hour

▲ Walking while brainstorming a project with your coworker

Recreational and Leisure Activities

▲ Badminton

▲ Billiards or pool

▲ Boating

- ▲ Bowling
- ▲ Canoeing (slow)
- ▲ Croquet
- ▲ Cycling (slow)
- ▲ Dancing
- ▲ Fishing
- ▲ Hiking (no load)
- ▲ Swimming (slow)
- ▲ Walking (3 mph)
- ▲ Table tennis

Strategies for Adding More Activity to Your Day

Here are some useful tips:

Make an appointment with yourself. Writing down a specific time and place for your activity in your planner or appointment book makes a big difference. It helps to know exactly when you're going to walk, run, or swim.

If you make activity a priority, you will be a happier, more energetic person.

Include family and friends. Using your activity as a time to be with family or friends can make it not only more pleasurable, but more likely that you will continue to do it.

Remember "accumulate" and "moderate." Find ways that you can accumulate small bursts of activity throughout the day. Also, don't make it too strenuous. Moderate activity is all that is necessary to derive almost all of the health benefits.

Vary your activity. Variety is the spice of life, and this holds true of activity. Vary your activity to keep it fresh and interesting.

Be prepared. Have the right equipment. This can be a good pair of walking shoes or an all-weather suit for damp or cold weather. If you have to wear dress shoes to work, keep a pair of walking shoes in the office. Pack your walking shoes for a business trip. Book your overnight business in a hotel with an indoor pool or fitness room.

Make it fun. Don't get stuck doing someone else's activity program. Find things that you enjoy doing and particularly those that can be fun with the family.

Seize the day. From time to time most of us suffer from procrastination. If you always think about ways you can fit more activity into your day, you are more likely to do it.

Prioritize. Remember, you are worth it! Even though there are many other demands on your life, if you make activity a priority, you will be a happier, more energetic person and can do a better job with the multiple tasks that you need to do every day.

Reward yourself. Give yourself credit for having the courage to go out and get more activity. After the first week, buy yourself a new CD to celebrate your increased activity. After the first month, perhaps splurge on an MP3 player. You get the point: Give yourself credit for increasing your activity.

Building a More Active Lifestyle

As you begin your quest for more regular activity, remember that it's not necessary to turn your life upside down. Just take small steps. I've already mentioned that the Balanced Walking Program starts with a ten-minute walk.

It's best to build physical activity in sequence. Unless you are currently engaged in a regular aerobic activity (such as a walking, jogging, cycling, or swimming program) at least three days a week, start with aerobics and not strength training. As you begin your walking or other aerobic activity, you will begin to use some of the stretches in the Balanced Flexibility Program. When your walking/aerobic activity is well established, you can begin either strength or flexibility training or both. You can also use the physical activity

programs online at StartMakingChoices.com, which will provide an online calendar for your activities and a personal tracking log.

Take a look at the activity section of your Balanced Life Index. Let's start by looking at the first two questions.

▲ *On a typical day, how much total incidental activity did you accumulate?*

▲ *How many days in the last week did you engage in a planned physical activity such as walking, jogging, or swimming?*

If you answered less than thirty minutes a day to accumulating activity and less than three days for planned activity, then you need to start with these goals:

▲ Find ways to be more active during each day.

▲ Begin a regular walking program (or other aerobic program), or expand your current program to at least three days a week.

If you are already doing strength training or flexibility activity—such as calisthenics, using hand weights or resistance bands, or weight training using machines or free weights—then you need to add an aerobic activity. Resistance training does not typically build adequate fitness. Also, depending on your workout program, you may be neglecting flexibility. Your activity program should contain aerobic, strength, and flexibility activities.

If you are already doing disciplines such as Pilates or yoga, you are typically building both strength and flexibility (not to mention gaining many mind-body and well-being benefits). Many Pilates and yoga programs, however, don't raise the heart rate high enough or long enough to build adequate cardiovascular fitness. I recommend adding regular walking or another aerobic activity. Aerobics training plus activities such as Pilates or yoga form a well-rounded activity program.

If you are already doing all three, that's terrific. In this case, check your BLI scores to see if there are areas that you need to strengthen. If you answered either 50 or 70 to all questions, keep up the good work, reward yourself, and go to work on nutrition and well-being. Otherwise, make some notes for where you want to tweak for improvement.

Before we go on to look at the various options for your activity plan, note your major priority on your goal-setting worksheet at the end of this chapter.

Making It Real: How One Couple Added More Physical Activity

Stacy and Mike are parents of a 9-year-old boy and a 7-year-old girl. Both have full-time jobs, volunteer at church, and manage the multiple activities of their children. As a result of all of these demands on their time, Stacy and Mike were never able to commit to a regular physical activity program. Though they tried to walk at least twice a week as a family, they felt that more cardio activity and strength training would give them stamina for their busy lives. When they took the BLI, they were surprised to realize that they were averaging three hours a night in front of the television or on the computer. On the BLI activity section, both scored in the low 100s.

Your activity program should contain aerobic, strength, and flexibility activities.

Stacy and Mike decided to work as a couple to increase their physical activity. First, they made a concerted effort to accumulate more incidental activity. Mike started parking in a garage two blocks farther from his office. Second, they started the Balanced Walking Program and gradually built up to walking four or five days a week. They also added seasonal activities that they could do with their children, such as bicycling and swimming. They added the Balanced

Strength-Training Program in the fourth month of their campaign. They increased their flexibility exercises by adding the Balanced Flexibility Program in month five.

After five months, Stacy and Mike's BLI activity scores rose into the upper 200s, moving them into the excellent balance category. Their overall BLI scores increased from the mid 600s to the high 700s, right on the cusp of moving from good balance into excellent balance. Mike was surprised at how easy it was to fit these minor changes into his life. He also found that being more physically active relieved his stress. Stacy discovered that being active helped her sleep better at night. Encouraged by their success, Stacy and Mike chose to work toward better balance in well-being as their next family challenge.

Aerobic Activity

For most people who undertake a regular program, fitness walking is an excellent aerobic activity. In research studies involving thousands of people, more than 80 percent see significant improvements in their cardiovascular fitness simply through fitness walking.

Walking carries the tremendous virtues of being comfortable, requiring little equipment, and being something that you can fit into almost any part of your day.

Why Call It Cardiovascular Fitness?

As we regularly do aerobic exercise, our entire cardiovascular system, not just the heart but also the arteries and veins and the interlinked pulmonary system, adapt to meet the challenges. As a result, our ability to do activity increases. It is this increase in our capacity to do exercise that improves our "cardiovascular fitness." We care about cardiovascular fitness because its levels are highly predictive of overall health. If your cardiovascular system is out of shape and poorly conditioned, you are at much greater risk of many health problems.

Other Forms of Aerobic Exercise

I recommend walking as your primary aerobic exercise—if you have been sedentary, you need to start slowly, and walking is gentle on your joints and easy to do. For the vast majority of people, walking carries the tremendous virtues of being comfortable, requiring very little equipment, and being something that you can fit into almost any part of your day. But many other forms of aerobic exercise will also give you multiple health benefits. For variety you may wish to use a second or third activity instead of walking, a practice which is called cross training. Or you may wish to substitute a different activity altogether for walking.

Jogging. Jogging is an excellent way to improve cardiovascular fitness—and you can do it just about anywhere. You may want to mix and match it with other activities such as swimming and walking. It is important to warm up and stretch properly. Jogging puts more pressure on the bones and joints than walking, so a good pair of well-padded jogging shoes (they are not the same as good walking shoes) is essential to minimize the impact and injury potential. If you are just beginning a regular activity program, work up to jogging. Don't begin to jog until you can walk at least thirty minutes at a brisk pace four or five days a week.

Cycling. Riding, whether outdoors or indoors on a stationary cycle, is an excellent form of cardiovascular exercise with very low impact. Some people find a racing-type bicycle uncomfortable because it requires leaning over to reach the handlebars. However, you can find lightweight road bikes with straight bars or upright bars that require little or no leaning over—or you may prefer riding a mountain bike on trails. Bikes are lighter and the shifting mechanism is much easier than many of us recall from our childhood days.

If you are cycling outdoors, always wear a helmet. Helmets could prevent an estimated 85 percent of cyclists' fatalities caused by head injuries. If you buy a stationary bicycle, chose a comfortable one that is easy to use—you may want to visit a health club to try them out.

You can also find ones that connect to computers with programs that not only monitor your output but also let you "see" yourself riding on various terrains.

Swimming. Swimming is an excellent upper and lower body exercise. Because the water supports your weight, swimming is very low impact. Water also provides resistance, which helps you build strength as well as fitness. For true fitness benefits, you need a certain degree of skill—but you could always take swimming lessons. And many people do not have access to a good swimming pool, such as a local high school, fitness club, YMCA, or college. Having to travel a long distance to a pool can seriously decrease the likelihood of your sticking with this form of exercise.

Elliptical trainers. The elliptical trainer is a relatively new type of exercise equipment that is a cross between walking and cycling. You stand in an upright position and pedal a circular pedal or move steps that travel in an elliptical pattern. These are excellent, low-impact forms of aerobic conditioning.

Rowing, cross-country skiing, and their machine equivalents. Both rowing and cross country skiing are excellent aerobic activities that are also superb total body conditioners. If you're near a lake or cross-country trails and have the skills to do these sports, these are great activities. Rowing and ski machines replicate the motions of the sports fairly well, but poorly designed machines can put you at greater risk of injury—so ask for advice at health clubs, or do some online research before buying.

Others. Other forms of aerobic activity include aerobic dancing, inline skating, and skateboarding. All of these activities use the large muscle groups in a repetitive fashion. Pick the one you enjoy the most, or better yet, pick a group of them and vary from day to day. This will keep your aerobic exercise program fresh.

YOUR AEROBIC PLAN:
The Balanced Walking Program

We all know that walking is basically simple. After all, we have all been doing it since we were babies! However, a few instructions will maximize your benefit and make walking even easier.

The Balanced Walking Program's easy-to-use calendar helps you progress from a sedentary to an active lifestyle in which you are walking briskly for thirty minutes on at least five days per week. If you already walk more than ten minutes on most days, start with the week closest to your activity level. You can also adapt the program to other physical activities.

Equipment needed: Walking shoes and comfortable, weather-appropriate clothing.

Convenience tip: If you don't wish to walk outdoors during poor weather (hot, rainy, frigid, snowy), locate convenient indoor locales where you can walk, such as a mall, or plan to cross-train with indoor cycling, swimming, or the like.

Using the Program

1. **Start slowly.** If you have not been following a formal program of activity, I recommend that you start with week one. If you are already walking regularly, pick the week level that matches your current activity. You can move forward or back as needed.

2. **Intensity.** The first column lists the intensity level for each week's walk. "Light" indicates a walking pace that is faster than a stroll but does not push you; this pace is probably close to your normal, everyday pace. "Moderate" intensity is a notch or two above "light"; your breathing and perception of exertion are increased but you should be able to talk normally. "Brisk" is a notch or two above "moderate"; your breathing rate and perception of exertion are elevated but you should not be breathless.

3. **Warm up and cool down.** Always begin your walk (or activity session) by warming up, and end it by cooling down. To warm up, simply walk at a light pace for three to four minutes before your session, and cool down the same way. After you start the stretching program, you may also use it to warm up and cool down.

The Balanced Walking Program

Minutes of Walking Per Day

Week	Intensity	Mon	Tue	Wed	Thur	Fri	Sat	Sun
1	light	10		10		10		
2	light-moderate	10		10		10		
3	light-moderate	12		12		12	(10)	
4	moderate	12		12		12	(12)	
5	moderate	15		12		15	(12)	
6	moderate	15		15		15		(15)
7	moderate-brisk	15		15	(12)	15		
8	moderate-brisk	15		15		15	15	
9	moderate-brisk	18		18		18		15
10	brisk	15		18		18	15	
11	brisk	18		18		18		18
12	brisk	20		18		20		18
13	brisk	20		20	(15)	20		20
14	brisk	20		22		20	22	
15	brisk	22		22	(20)	22		22
16	brisk	25		22		25	(20)	22
17	brisk	25		25	20	25		25
18	brisk	25		27		25		27
19	brisk	27	(25)	30		27		30
20	brisk	30		30	30	30		30

All sessions in parentheses ( ) are optional.

You may vary days of the week for walking sessions; simply maintain the every-other-day pattern of the calendar.

To increase session duration beyond 30 minutes, continue gradually increasing minutes, but no more than 10 to 20 percent per week.

Adapting the Walking Program for Other Activities

For variety you may choose to alternate other activities such as cycling or swimming with walking. Or perhaps you prefer an alternate primary activity. Here are tips for adapting the calendar:

Cycling (outdoor): For cycling on level terrain, increase times by five minutes—so you'd start out by cycling fifteen minutes rather than ten. For cycling on hilly terrain, decrease times by five minutes or take one-minute breaks within the session as needed

Cycling (stationary indoor): Use the same duration for sessions, and gradually increase the resistance setting to simulate a moderate to brisk pace.

Elliptical trainers: Elliptical trainers vary widely in the features they offer. Use the times of the training calendar, and gradually increase either resistance or incline each week to maintain the level of intensity indicated.

Jogging: Jogging is a high-impact activity that can stress your joints. Do not begin jogging until you can briskly walk thirty minutes four or five days a week, and use good running shoes. Begin jogging gradually. A good way to start is by jogging for one minute (or one hundred steps), then walking two minutes (or two hundred steps). Gradually add time or steps. Continue to take walking breaks as needed. Do not run through pain.

Rowing and ski machines: Decrease the time indicated by five minutes per session or take rest breaks: row five minutes, rest one, row five. Repeat each week's level twice.

Swimming: Use the same duration, but when you start, do not try to swim ten minutes continuously. Swim five minutes, rest one, swim five. Increase the duration of your continuous swim gradually. Repeat a week's pattern as necessary. The recommended stroke for fitness swimming is freestyle. You may also vary strokes.

Treadmills: Treadmills vary widely in the features they offer. Use the times of the training calendar; gradually increase either the speed or incline each week to maintain the level of intensity indicated.

Strength Training

Once aerobic activity has become a part of your daily routine, you can add strength exercises and flexibility exercises to balance your overall functional fitness.

Strength training, particularly in combination with aerobic training, is one of the best health decisions you can make. However, very few people do strength training—probably less than 5 percent of the adult population in the United States. I think it is because most people think they would have to lift heavy weights or do body building and make frequent gym visits. But we can all strength train, and we can do it at home. The benefits are enormous.

The Multiple Benefits of Strength Training

Maintaining or building strong, flexible muscles yields many benefits for every adult. Research on the benefits of strength exercise is so overwhelming that by the 1990s, the American College of Sports Medicine revised its exercise recommendations to include both strength training and aerobic exercise as part of an overall approach to healthy living.

People who do both aerobic conditioning and strength training can increase their lean muscle mass while losing large amounts of fat.

Maintains lean muscle tissue. Unless we are physically active and give our muscles a workout, as we age we tend to lose lean muscle tissue. Strength training maintains and builds muscle mass, keeping your metabolism high and boosting functional fitness.

Controls weight. Strength training can help with weight control. Our research lab has found that people who do both aerobic conditioning and strength training can increase their lean muscle mass while losing large amounts of fat. Without regular activity, many people actually lose lean muscle mass as they lose weight and thereby decrease metabolism. This makes regaining the weight much more likely.

Promotes bone health and slows osteoporosis. Many studies show that people (particularly women) who regularly engage in strength training have stronger bones and less osteoporosis.

Helps prevent injuries. Having strong and flexible muscles decreases the likelihood of injuring yourself, either during your activities of daily living or during recreational activities.

Improves physical appearance. People with strong, flexible muscles carry themselves better, sometimes with better posture, and in general have an improved physical appearance.

Strength-training exercises should achieve an intensity that will cause near muscle fatigue as you reach the end of the exercise set.

Improves self-esteem. Our research lab has shown improved mood and self-esteem for people who strength train. Being strong and having well-conditioned muscles can also increase your confidence. Conversely, having weaker muscles can contribute to depression.

Improves physical performance. A stronger body helps improve your performance both in daily activities and in recreational sports. Some years ago, we followed a woman on the professional women's golf tour and prescribed strength exercises for her during the off-season. In that short time, she was able to increase the yardage on her drives over twenty-five yards! This type of improvement is consistent with the kind of results that we have seen in many studies.

Strength-Training Guidelines

On the following the pages are some guidelines to help you achieve the maximum benefits with the greatest safety.

Warm up and cool down. A good warm-up and cool-down are essential for the efficiency and safety of a strength-training program. Stretching should be part of both warm-up and cool-down; you can use appropriate stretches from the Balanced Flexibility Program later in this chapter. Your warm-up and cool-down should also include some light exercise for three to five minutes before and after your strength-training workout. Walking or cycling slowly is sufficient.

Selecting the right exercises. A balanced strength-training program includes exercises that strengthen all of the body's major muscle groups. Your body has ten major muscle groups: abdominal, lower back (rector spinates), chest (pectorals), upper back (rhomboids and trapezius), biceps, shoulders (deltoids), triceps, neck, front of thigh (quadriceps), and rear thigh (hamstrings). The strength program in this book and the programs on StartMakingChoices.com are designed to exercise all these muscle groups.

Working at the right intensity. For best results, strength-training exercises should achieve an intensity that will cause near muscle fatigue as you reach the end of each exercise set—this means at the point where you can barely lift the weight. The Balanced Strength Program achieves this intensity by gradually increasing repetitions.

Selecting exercise speed. You should do the movements of each exercise slowly enough that you can control them throughout the whole range of motion. Working slowly under control benefits the muscles the most and reduces the chance of injury from out-of-control motions.

Using the muscles' full range. Every muscle has a range where it is strongest. However, you should do each exercise so that you can use the right technique throughout the full range of motion for the muscle. If you can only lift a weight through a short arc of the muscle, you are lifting too much weight.

Strength-training frequency. According to the American College of Sports Medicine, the optimum frequency for strength-training exercises is two to three times a week with at least one day off between. If you want to do strength training more often than this, I recommend alternating, doing upper body exercises one day and lower body exercises the next day.

Progression. The Balanced Strength Program is calisthenics-based and uses a few light hand and ankle weights. Progression, or increasing resistance, is achieved by increasing the number of repetitions. This is built into your training calendar. If you are using barbells or machines to do the programs on StartMakingChoices.com, I recommend double progression. This alternately increases the weight or number of repetitions. If you are using an exercise machine, you might start with ten repetitions of fifteen pounds. You would stay with the fifteen pounds until you felt comfortable up to twelve repetitions. Then you would increase to sixteen or seventeen pounds and drop back to ten repetitions. Do not advance either repetitions or weight too quickly! This is the most common mistake that most people make. Normally, as you are beginning, your strength will increase 2 to 5 percent a week with a well-structured strength-training program.

Breathing. It is important that you not hold your breath during strength-training exercises—this can result in temporary, but dangerous, increases in blood pressure. Instead, comfortably breathe out when you are lifting the weight (your body or part of your body may be the weight) and breathe in when you are putting it down.

Safety. If you have any significant medical problem, please check with your physician before starting any program. Never use any exercise equipment you are unfamiliar with, and always start with low weights to determine where you are comfortable.

In addition to following all the guidelines listed here, you may want to find a qualified personal trainer or health club professional to help you get started. This person can help you select the proper equipment, develop a routine, and teach you proper technique.

YOUR STRENGTH-TRAINING PLAN:
Balanced Strength Program

The exercises for the Balanced Strength Program are based on calisthenics, which you can easily do at home. This approach means that the weight, or resistance, that you work against is primarily the weight of your body. Only three exercises use small hand weights. As you progress, you may add additional hand weights and leg weights if you wish.

Warm up and cool down before and after each session using the stretches in the Flexibility Program beginning on page 102 and three to five minutes of light exercise (such as stationary cycling or walking).

Clothing: Loose-fitting comfortable clothing and athletic shoes.

Equipment: A carpeted floor or exercise mat; a sturdy straight-back chair; one-pound, two-pound, and three-pound pairs of dumbbells, available in sporting goods departments and stores.

Optional for later: Adjustable leg weights, one to ten pounds

More information: Go to StartMakingChoices.com for more information on how to do these strength-training exercises, illustrations, and video clips.

Upper Body Exercises

A. Good Morning Exercise. Stand with feet slightly wider than shoulder-width apart. Keeping your back straight and arms spread wide or on your hips, bend the hips/waist until your torso is parallel to the floor; then return to starting position. When your torso is parallel to the floor, your head should be up, looking directly in front of you. You should feel this exercise in the lower back and hamstrings.

B. Push-ups or Modified Push-ups. Place hands shoulder-width apart on floor and the balls of your feet on the floor behind you. Keeping your back straight (using your abdominal/back musculature), lower yourself until your waist touches the floor. Return to starting position.

If you cannot do the standard push-up, use the same position but start on your knees, with knees bent so calves are at a right angle to thighs. Be sure to use an exercise mat if you work from your knees.

If the modified push-up is too difficult or you can't rest on your knees, you may start with a wall push-up. You need a clear area of wall with no obstacles and firm footing. Position your feet a comfortable arm's length from the wall and shoulder-width apart. Place your hands, palms out, against the wall at shoulder width and height. Pivoting on the balls of your feet (don't move them) and keeping your back and neck straight, lower your chest/head toward the wall. Return to starting position. When you can manage this easily, shift your feet farther away from the wall in two-inch increments, but no farther than six inches total. When you can do these wall push-ups easily, shift to regular push-ups.

C. Biceps Curls. Start by standing in a comfortable position with your arms at your sides, palms facing forward. Keeping your upper arm straight and close to your body, flex at the elbow until your elbow points directly downward. You may do this exercise without weight for the first stage or begin with one-pound dumbbells and progress slowly.

D. Shoulder Raises. In a standing position with your arms at your sides and palms facing the outside of your legs, raise arms straight out to the side until they are parallel to the floor. Slowly return to starting position. You may do this exercise without weight for the first stage or begin with one-pound dumbbells and progress slowly.

E. Triceps Extensions. In a standing position, grasp a one- or two-pound dumbbell weight in both hands and extend your arms straight up above your head. Keeping your upper arms from shoulder to elbow vertical, lower the dumbbell toward the back until your elbows are flexed fully. Return to vertical starting position.

F. Abdominal Crunches. Lie on a mat or carpeted floor. Lift your legs off the floor and bend at the knees so that your legs form a right angle, with your lower legs parallel to the floor. Keeping your lower back on the floor, curl up until your shoulder blades come off the floor, and return to starting position. This exercise should be done very slowly with your arms crossed on your chest or at your sides; do not lock your hands behind your neck. It may be helpful to squeeze a ball or towel gently between your knees to better target your abdominal muscles.

Lower Body Exercises

A. Squats. Stand with your feet shoulder-width apart and pointed slightly outward. Keeping your back straight and head upright, sit slightly backward and lower yourself to a comfortable position, using your arms to balance yourself. Your knees should always remain directly above your feet and never in front of your toes. Keep your head up during the entire movement and never look down to check your form (use a mirror if necessary). If your knees are too far forward as you squat, sit farther back when beginning the exercise. Your feet should remain flat on the floor at all times, never up on your toes.

B. Knee Extension. Get on your hands and knees, and lift one leg so that it is straight out behind you. Flex the raised leg at the knee, moving your heel toward your buttock until your upper and lower legs touch. Your heel should be slightly beyond vertical; it does not touch your buttock. Don't force the flex. Return slowly to starting position. Complete the exercise for one leg and then the other, or alternate sets. Beginning in Stage 3, this exercise can be done with ankle weights.

C. Lunges. Stand with your feet about six to eight inches apart. Take a step forward that is slightly larger than usual, and with your back straight, lower your opposite knee slowly to the floor. Push forcefully upward from this position, returning to starting position. Alternate legs for this exercise.

D. Hip Abduction (Side Leg Raises). Lie on the floor on your side with your feet together. Keeping your body straight, raise your leg out from your side to a comfortable position, then slowly return to starting position. Use the floor to help keep your balance while your leg is in the air. Do this exercise for both legs in turn. Starting in Stage 3, you may use ankle weights.

E. Hip Extension. Lean over a table (on your forearms/elbows) with your legs straight and close together. Slowly raise your leg behind you and away from the table until it is parallel, or almost parallel, to the floor, then slowly return to starting position. Do this for both legs in turn. Starting in Stage 3, you may use ankle weights.

F. Calf Raises. Stand facing a wall or chair back with your feet together and knees slightly bent (unlocked). While holding on to the wall or chair for balance, rise on your toes (both feet at the same time) and slowly sink back down to the floor.

If you split your regimen and do upper body work one day and lower body work another day, do the exercises in the order listed:

Upper Body Exercises
A. Good morning exercise
B. Push-ups/Modified push-ups
C. Biceps curls
D. Shoulder raises
E. Triceps extensions
F. Abdominal crunches

Lower Body Exercises
A. Squats
B. Knee extension
C. Lunges
D. Hip abduction (side leg raises)
E. Hip extension
F. Calf Raises

If you do both upper and lower body regimens at the same workout session, do the exercises in pairs: Upper A, then Lower A; Upper B, then Lower B; and so forth.

Do the exercises in order for the indicated sets and repetitions (reps). A set is a group of repetitions. Rest no less than fifteen seconds and no more than a minute-and-a-half between sets. Rest only two or three minutes between exercises. If you find that the week one routine is too light, you may skip to week seven and begin there.

Frequency Options

1 . *Two or three times weekly.* Do both upper and lower body exercises on the same day. Rest for at least one day between training sessions.
2. *Four times weekly.* Do upper body exercises on Mondays and Thursdays and lower body exercises on Tuesdays and Fridays. Take Wednesday and weekends off.
3. *Six times weekly.* Do upper and lower body exercises on alternate days. Rest on the day following your third consecutive day of working out.

Stage 1 Program

Week 1:	1 set/ 10 reps	
Week 2:	1 set/ 11 reps	
Week 3:	1 set/ 12 reps	
Week 4:	1 set/ 10 reps	plus 1 set/ 3 reps
Week 5:	1 set/ 10 reps	plus 1 set/ 4 reps
Week 6:	1 set/ 10 reps	plus 1 set/ 5 reps
Week 7:	1 set/ 10 reps	plus 1 set/ 6 reps
Week 8:	1 set/ 10 reps	plus 1 set/ 7 reps
Week 9:	1 set/ 10 reps	plus 1 set/ 8 reps
Week 10:	1 set/ 10 reps	plus 1 set/ 9 reps
Week 11:	1 set/ 10 reps	plus 1 set/ 10 reps
Week 12:	1 set/ 10 reps	plus 1 set/ 10 reps

Stage 2 Program

Week 13:	2 sets/ 10 reps	
Week 14:	2 sets/ 11 reps	
Week 15:	2 sets/ 12 reps	
Week 16:	2 sets/ 10 reps	plus 1 set/ 5 reps
Week 17:	2 sets/ 10 reps	plus 1 set/ 6 reps
Week 18:	2 sets/ 10 reps	plus 1 set/ 7 reps
Week 19:	2 sets/ 10 reps	plus 1 set/ 8 reps

Week 20:	2 sets/ 10 reps	plus 1 set/ 9 reps
Week 21:	2 sets/ 10 reps	plus 1 set/ 10 reps
Week 22:	1 set/ 11 reps	plus 2 sets/ 10 reps
Week 23:	2 sets/ 11 reps	plus 1 set/ 10 reps
Week 24:	3 sets/ 11 reps	

Stage 3 Program

Week 25:	3 sets/ 10-12 reps/ no weight	
Week 26:	1 set/ 10 reps/ 1 lb weight	plus 2 sets/ 10 reps/ no weight
Week 27:	2 sets/ 10 reps/ 1 lb weight	plus 1 set/10 reps/ no weight
Week 28:	3 sets/ 10 reps/ 1 lb weight	
Week 29:	1 set/ 10 reps/ 2 lb weight	plus 2 sets/ 10 reps/ 1 lb weight
Week 30:	2 sets/ 10 reps/ 2 lb weight	plus 1 set/ 10 reps/ 1 lb weight
Week 31:	3 sets/ 10 reps/ 2 lb weight	
Week 32:	1 set/ 10 reps/ 3 lb weight	plus 2 sets/ 10 reps/ 2 lb weight
Week 33:	2 sets/ 10 reps/ 3 lb weight	plus 1 set/ 10 reps/ 2 lb weight
Week 34:	3 sets/ 10 reps/ 3 lb weight	
Week 35:	1 set/ 10 reps/ 4 lb weight	plus 2 sets/ 10 reps/ 3 lb weight
Week 36:	2 sets/ 10 reps/ 4 lb weight	plus 1 set/ 10 reps/ 3 lb weight
Week 37:	3 sets/ 10 reps/ 4 lb weight	

At the end of week 37, you may maintain this level, or you may continue to add weights in this progressive pattern until you reach five pounds for the upper body regimen and ten pounds for the lower body regimen.

If you would like to do an equivalent workout on machines, you can find an excellent program that includes animated illustrations of the exercises at StartMakingChoices.com.

Building Flexibility

Flexibility exercise is the third of the three types of exercise forming the upper wedges of the Balanced Activity Pyramid. Flexibility is underrated as a major component of maintaining healthy muscles and joints. Often people start their exercise program without any stretching either before or after. Mistake!

Stretching, either as a separate exercise program, or before and after each aerobic and strength-training session, is important for many reasons. It not only lowers your risk of injury during exercise, but stretching daily will assure that you maintain the highest possible level of range of motion in your joints.

Stretching gives you an opportunity to focus on mind-body issues that benefit the overall balance in your exercise program.

Stretching also gives you an opportunity to focus on mind-body issues that benefit the overall balance in your exercise program. Take a little time daily to get in tune with your body, lower your risk of injury, and help balance your activity program and life. So whether you have a separate time for a daily stretching program, engage in Pilates, yoga, or tai chi, or simply use your stretching program before and after aerobic exercise and/or strength exercise, you're making the right move! You may start a flexibility program either before or independent of a strength-training program.

The Many Benefits of Increased Flexibility

Flexibility is the ability to move your joints easily in order to meet the challenges of daily life. It offers many benefits:

Injury prevention. Increased flexibility contributes to injury prevention by improving balance and preventing over-stretching, which may injure muscles or tendons. Poor balance is a major cause of falls.

Many injuries from over-stretching (hyperextension) happen during a normal day when you misstep or reach too far while doing a chore around the house or office.

Improved performance. Good flexibility allows you to rotate through a full range of motion. This improves your performance whether you are trimming shrubbery, cleaning the gutters, driving a golf ball, or smashing a tennis serve.

Building strength. Some types of stretching are valuable for building strength as well as flexibility. For example, yoga and Pilates are not only great stretching exercises but also build strong healthy muscles.

Mind/body benefits. I always use my stretching program as a time to get in touch with my body. During the gentle stretching motions, there is time to relax and get in tune with your body. Many people really enjoy this quality most, particularly with such gentle exercises as tai chi and many forms of yoga.

Slowing the aging process. Maintaining an active lifestyle is one way that we can slow the physiologic process of aging. Flexibility training helps maintain such an active lifestyle. The older we get, the more regular stretching helps slow or even reverse age-related decreases in flexibility.

YOUR STRETCHING PLAN:
Balanced Flexibility Exercises

The stretching program is divided into upper and lower body exercises. Each exercise targets a specific major muscle group. Again, it is important to concentrate on what you are doing and to listen to what your body is telling you. Do the exercises in the order given.

Equipment: Loose comfortable clothing. Do the stretches barefoot or in sock feet; not wearing shoes assists in proper extension, particularly of ankles and feet.

Before you start: Begin with a light five-minute warm-up to increase circulation, warm up muscles, and generally prepare the body for the exercises. The warm-up can be light calisthenics, a brisk walk, jogging in place, or cycling.

During the exercise: It is essential to progress slowly and to be consistent with your program. Begin the program by holding each position for ten seconds. As you increase your flexibility and range of motion, hold the position for fifteen to twenty seconds. It is not necessary to do each exercise for more than twenty seconds. Do not force the extension or "bounce"; you could injure yourself.

After stretching: End your stretching exercise program with a cool-down, repeating the same warm-up activities, but at a slower pace, for an additional five to ten minutes.

More information: Go to StartMakingChoices.com for illustrations and video clips of these stretches and for additional information.

Upper Body Program

Full body stretch. Lying on your back, extend your arms straight over your head and your legs straight out (pointing your toes) in the opposite direction. Reach; extend and hold for ten seconds; relax. Repeat two or three times.

Full upper body stretch. Sitting, with legs bent underneath you, reach forward with both arms extended forward while pressing your palms to the floor. This can also be done one arm at a time. Reach for ten seconds; then relax. Repeat two or three times.

Shoulders and outer portions of arms and ribs. While sitting cross-legged or standing upright, extend your arms over your head, pull your palms together, and stretch your arms upward and slightly backward (behind your head). Hold for ten seconds; then relax. Repeat two or three times.

Shoulders and middle back. While sitting or standing, draw your arm across your chest toward the opposite shoulder by pushing in at your elbow with your other hand. You may flex the elbow of the extended arm. Do this on both the left and right sides. Hold each stretch for ten seconds, and then relax. Repeat two or three times with each arm.

Side stretch. While standing with knees slightly bent, extend your arms above your head and flex them over the top of your head. Use one hand to gently increase the extension toward one side of your head. In the same motion, bend from the hips to the same side (in the same direction you are gently pulling your elbow). Hold for ten seconds; then relax. Repeat two or three times on each side.

Shoulder and neck stretch. Leaning your head toward your right shoulder, pull your right arm down across behind your back with your left hand. Do this exercise on both sides, holding each stretch for ten seconds and then relaxing. Repeat two or three times on each side.

Arms, shoulders, and chest. Extend your arms back behind your back and clasp hands together. Then slowly pull your interlocked fingers upward. Hold for ten seconds, then relax. Repeat two or three times.

Lower Body Program

Calf stretch. Standing slightly away from a wall or a steady support, lean on it with your arms. Bend one leg, and keep the other leg slightly bent back behind you. Move your hips forward toward the wall while attempting to keep the heel of the back leg flat on the ground. Do the stretch on both sides, holding each stretch for ten to thirty seconds. Repeat two or three times on each side.

Groin stretch. While sitting on the floor with the balls of the feet together and the back straight, attempt to push your knees outward and toward the ground. Hold the position for ten seconds; then relax. Repeat two or three times, doing the exercise slowly because very little movement will elicit a stretch.

Hamstring stretch. While sitting with legs extended outward (slightly bent) and in the straddle position, bend forward at the hips, reach toward one leg, and hold. Then reach toward the middle, and hold; finally reach toward the opposite leg, and hold. Do this two or three times in each of the three positions, slowly and deliberately.

Quadriceps (thigh) stretch. Stretch One: Sitting with one leg extended outward and the other leg bent in the hurdler's position (with the foot pointing outward from the body), begin to lean slightly backward. Move slowly and deliberately since this exercise requires little movement to elicit a stretch response. Hold the position for ten seconds; then relax. Do this two or three times on each side. Stretch Two: With one knee resting on the floor and the other leg out in front (the knee of the front leg should be directly over the ankle), lower the front of your hip toward the floor slowly. Hold position for ten seconds; then relax. Do this exercise two or three times on the right and left sides.

Ankle rotation. While sitting cross-legged, roll one foot in a circle clockwise and counterclockwise. Do this exercise three or four times in each direction on both ankles.

Prioritizing and Tracking Your Activity Program

Turn to your goal-setting worksheets on the following pages and write down the steps you plan to take in order of priority. Give yourself a start date for the first activity.

Keeping track of your progress daily as you do activity is highly motivating. If you post your walking (or aerobic) calendar in your planner or on the fridge then you can check off each session as you do it. In the appendices you'll find some blank log sheets that you can use to record all your activity programs, particularly strength training and stretching. You can also use your log as a journal to record ideas or insights that help you keep going forward.

If you have Internet access, explore the online exercise information and personal activity planner available at StartMakingChoices.com. This interactive program lets you select activities you enjoy and can be set to increase in difficulty as you progress. You can even see proper exercise techniques using the included videos and illustrations. The site gives you instant feedback on how you are progressing each week against your goals. You can also read daily tips to enhance your program, and you can even read other users' blogs to learn about their experiences with StartMakingChoices.com.

It's also a good idea to check your progress regularly by retaking the Balanced Life Index, either using the form in this book or the online form if you are participating at StartMakingChoices.com. Once you've signed up online, StartMakingChoices.com will do the math for you. You can see your performance in real time and compare your BLI with others in the StartMakingChoices.com community.

Your Plan for a Balanced Life
Goal-Setting Worksheet: Aerobic Activity

Goal 1: _____

   Strategy: _____

      Action Steps: _____

   Strategy: _____

      Action Steps: _____

   Strategy: _____

      Action Steps: _____

Goal 2: _____

   Strategy: _____

      Action Steps: _____

   Strategy: _____

      Action Steps: _____

   Strategy: _____

      Action Steps: _____

Goal 3: _____

   Strategy: _____

      Action Steps: _____

   Strategy: _____

      Action Steps: _____

   Strategy: _____

      Action Steps: _____

Your Plan for a Balanced Life
Goal-Setting Worksheet: Strength Training

Goal 1: _____

    Strategy: _____

        Action Steps: _____

    Strategy: _____

        Action Steps: _____

    Strategy: _____

        Action Steps: _____

Goal 2: _____

    Strategy: _____

        Action Steps: _____

    Strategy: _____

        Action Steps: _____

    Strategy: _____

        Action Steps: _____

Goal 3: _____

    Strategy: _____

        Action Steps: _____

    Strategy: _____

        Action Steps: _____

    Strategy: _____

        Action Steps: _____

Your Plan for a Balanced Life
Goal-Setting Worksheet: Flexibility

Goal 1: _____

    Strategy: _____

        Action Steps: _____

    Strategy: _____

        Action Steps: _____

    Strategy: _____

        Action Steps: _____

Goal 2: _____

    Strategy: _____

        Action Steps: _____

    Strategy: _____

        Action Steps: _____

    Strategy: _____

        Action Steps: _____

Goal 3: _____

    Strategy: _____

        Action Steps: _____

    Strategy: _____

        Action Steps: _____

    Strategy: _____

        Action Steps: _____

Your Balanced Well-Being Plan

What does well-being mean in the context of a balanced life? Well-being is something of an umbrella term that I use to cover many aspects of our perceived quality of life. In this chapter I will break well-being into its major components and contributing lifestyle issues. You'll also find specific tools and tips to help you achieve more balance, happiness, and satisfaction.

The well-being pyramid contains the key components that we have discovered are vital to well-being and quality of life.

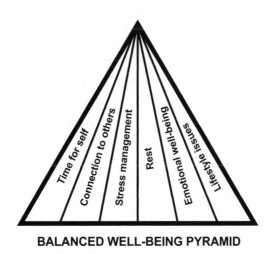

BALANCED WELL-BEING PYRAMID

As you can see, well-being is rooted in the connections among your mind, body, and spirit. Some of the elements of well-being that we will explore include:

▲ benefits found in managing stress
▲ benefits in connecting with others (which includes time for family and friends)
▲ taking time for yourself
▲ why rest is so critical to well-being
▲ how our emotions affect our well-being
▲ the importance of weight management
▲ the effects of smoking

How Balanced Is Your Approach to Well-Being?

Take a moment to look at your scores on the well-being section of your Balanced Life Index. How well are you doing overall? How well are you doing on the five elements: time you take for yourself, time you take for family and friends, how much stress affects your life, what your weight status is, and smoking?

As you consider your scores, think about which areas need the most work and make some notes on your goal-setting worksheet about your priorities. The following survey may help you organize your thoughts. For each well-being component listed in the first column, circle which response best describes you. Use your responses to prioritize which component(s) of well-being you want to tackle.

Time I take for myself	Improve somewhat	Improve a lot	Managing OK
Time with family and others	Improve somewhat	Improve a lot	Managing OK
Stress management	Improve somewhat	Improve a lot	Managing OK
Weight management	Need to lose weight	Satisfied with current weight	Need to gain weight
Smoking	Smoke more than a pack a day	Never smoked	Smoke less than a pack a day

You'll also consider other components of the well-being pyramid not directly measured by the BLI: the time you take for rest and the keys to emotional well-being. Keep your evaluations in mind and your goal-setting worksheet handy as you read through the sections on each component of well-being. Jot down strategies and techniques you think will work for you. You can also refer to StartMakingChoices.com for an easy-to-use well-being planner and to log your programs.

Taking Time for Yourself

If you are going to bring your whole self to the relationships and commitments that are important to you, then you must take time for yourself.

A woman I know in her sixties was going with small groups on extended wilderness treks far away from any towns or services. She was much older than most of her trekking companions, and one of the things she learned early in trekking was that her first responsibility was to take care of herself. If she had not trained hard to be fit and conditioned for the trek and if she did not have the proper equipment, then she was a liability to the group. She learned that her first responsibility to the well-being of the group was to take care of herself.

> *Our first responsibility to ourselves, to those we love, and to the work we value is to try to be our best.*

Our first responsibility to ourselves, to those we love, and to the work we value is to try to be our best. That means taking time for ourselves. It may be a daily walk or swim, writing a letter to a friend, or taking a stress-relieving ten-minute "time-out." It might be taking time to read, do needlework or woodworking, or sit and watch the sunset. You define what feeds your spirit. It might be something no one else would think of. A friend once told me that the quietest personal times of the day were the forty minutes morning and night spent commuting on the crowded subway from home to work and back. Over several years, she read dozens of the great books she'd always meant to find time for.

Think specifically about how you can find some time each day for yourself—and think about taking at least part of a day on a regular basis for yourself.

Connection to Others

> *No man is an island, entire of itself; every man is a piece of the continent, a part of the main. If a clod be washed away by the sea, Europe is the less, as well as if promontory were, as well as if a manor of thy friend's or of thine own were. Any man's death diminishes me, because I am involved in mankind; and therefore never send to know for whom the bell tolls; it tolls for thee.*

These words from John Donne's "Meditation XVII" have touched a chord with many people throughout the four centuries since they were written. Our ability to connect with others gives our life meaning, richness, and joy. Nurturing the relationships that give us vitality can help us feel balanced.

Family and Friends

When we ask patients to identify their sources of greatest satisfaction, the most frequent answer is "family." Family relationships can sometimes be difficult, but when families cherish their bond there is no greater support.

But sometimes we neglect spending time with our families. Think about your priorities. Are they as important as family? Can you make some adjustments so that you can reach out to family more often?

Studies have shown that people who are connected to their community or other people are healthier.

Thomas Jefferson said, "The most treasured times in my life were spent in the bosom of my family." I couldn't agree more. You may be able to increase time spent with your family by eating meals together, planning regular family outings such as picnics, movie nights, or educational events, or even working together as family on some of the necessary household chores.

Connecting with friends is also important. Friendship is personal and based on each friend caring for the welfare of the other. Usually friends have shared interests. In genuine friendships, friends make great listeners for each other; they challenge each other's thinking and encourage each other's dreams.

Studies have shown that people who are connected to their community or other people are healthier. A five-year study by Dr. Redford Williams at Duke University followed more than 1,400 men and women who were undergoing heart catheterization because of significant narrowing of at least one coronary artery.[1] At the end of the study, people who were not married or did not have at least one close confidante were three times as likely to have died as those who had close connections to other people. Many other studies have shown similar findings.

Finding another place where you can engage and share hopes, dreams, and aspirations with other like-minded people can greatly enrich your life.

These days many people spend a lot of time making "connections" on the Internet. The burgeoning opportunities of our increasingly "wired" world suggest that many people should find it easier to establish a community. Unfortunately, just the opposite appears to be true. In 1985, the average person in the United States had three people to whom they could confide important matters. By 2004, this had dropped to two close confidantes and 25 percent had no close confidantes.[2] When it comes to establishing community, personal touch and presence appear to be critically important.

Volunteering

People who volunteer and who do good for others get multiple benefits themselves! Studies suggest that volunteers have higher self-esteem, lower blood pressure, less insomnia, and a better immune system than those who don't volunteer. Volunteering is also associated with greater longevity. In one study of people who had been laid off from work, those who volunteered during their time of unemployment were more likely to find a job than those who didn't volunteer.[3]

Why does volunteering offer all these benefits? It appears that the act of doing good for other people fills a deep-seated human need to connect and to care.

Every community offers many opportunities to volunteer. You can match your skills and interests to the needs of your community. It may seem difficult to volunteer in the midst of an already busy life, but it's a gift that gives back, bringing you health benefits and balance.

Finding a Third Place

Each of us has one or two "places." For most of us, these are home and work. However, finding another place where you can engage and share hopes, dreams, and aspirations with other like-minded people can greatly enrich your life. This might be a health club, religious organization, civic club, bookstore, or gatherings such as the networks of collectors who spend their weekends at flea markets. In a third place you can connect to other people and share interests and passions that may have no outlet at home or at work.

Think about what your third place might be, and work to satisfy that need that your soul has to connect with other people who are like-minded.

Our ability to reach out and connect with other people is vitally important to achieving balance and well-being in our lives.

Sharing with Others

Early in my career, I was recruited to be chief of staff of a Midwestern hospital. The retiring chief of medicine, Jack, and his wife invited me for a weekend at their country farm, which included a trout stream. Jack was an avid trout fisherman, but I had never trout fished. Jack was patient with me, teaching me the techniques of casting the fly and reeling in the fish. At the end of the day, a bit embarrassed by my clumsiness, I said to Jack, "Thanks for spending all that time with me. I know I am not very good at fly fishing, but I certainly appreciate that you shared this with me."

He turned to me and said something that I have never forgotten. "No, Jim, I thank you. It was a great day for me. There is nothing more pleasurable than teaching someone something that you love." Jack's generosity to me is a wonderful example of sharing with others.

I strive to emulate Jack's generosity of spirit as I work with young researchers and physicians. Teaching or sharing something you love is one of the great joys of being a parent, grandparent, a volunteer. It's another way to connect to others, and a key to sharing between generations of people.

Our ability to reach out and connect with other people is vitally important to achieving balance and well-being in our lives. Take time to reach out to others and you'll be energized and uplifted by participating in the circle of life.

Managing Stress

Defining stress may be a little like that old joke about defining art: You may not be able to define it, but you know it when you experience it. Perhaps the best definition of stress came more than half a century ago, from a Canadian researcher named Hans Selye. In his classic 1956 book, *The Stress of Life*, Dr. Selye defined stress as the nonspecific response of the body to any demand made upon it.[4]

Stress is unavoidable, but our reaction to it is not.

This simple definition includes both of the key components of stress. Specifically, stress involves a demand (which often comes from the outside) as well as our response (which often comes from the inside). In our daily lives, we face many demands from our daily activities, our children, our jobs, and the greater world around us.

Why Do We Care about Stress?

Uncontrolled stress exposes us to risks. These risks include:

Diminished quality of life. Continuous unremitting stress makes for a miserable life, eroding day-to-day emotional well-being.

The disease connection. Stress has been linked to a wide variety of diseases ranging from heart disease to the common cold. Substantial scientific evidence connects stress to heart rhythm disturbances, chest pains, and even narrowing of the coronary arteries. Stress has also been clearly connected to an increased prevalence of high blood pressure, a major risk factor for both heart disease and stroke. People with a high level of stress, particularly chronic stress, are more likely to develop colds than those with lower levels of stress.[5]

Practicing living in the present every day will lower the background stress that clutters daily life.

Damage to performance. Uncontrolled stress takes charge of our lives and damages performance. Several studies report that from 26 to 40 percent of people state that the stress of their work affects how they feel and perform.[6]

Stress is unavoidable, but our reaction to it is not. If we have adequate coping skills, if we know the steps to manage or reduce its impact, then we can protect ourselves from many of its dangers. But if we allow stress to trigger toxic reactions such as anger or hostility, our response not only increases the impact of the original stress but becomes a source of additional stress. Fortunately, we can learn to manage stress.

A Three-Point Plan for Stress Management

All successful stress reduction plans boil down to a simple strategy: learn to live in the present, and develop a specific plan for stress relief that works for you.

Articulating this strategy is simple; putting it in action is more difficult. I devised a simple rhyme to remind me of the key steps in my stress management plan:

▲ Seize the day
▲ Get out of your own way
▲ Make a personal play

Seize the day! I lifted that from the ancient Romans' *Carpe diem!* In English we might say, "Strike while the iron is hot" or "Don't let the grass grow under your feet." By seize the day, I mean live in the present. I also mean *do it now and practice it daily.* Most of us spend too much time regretting the past or fearing the future. Practicing living in the present every day will lower the background stress that clutters daily life and will also let you "seize the day" when more acutely stressful events occur. (Living in the present doesn't mean that you quit planning and preparing—that's part of what you do to decrease stress.)

Activity burns a lot of the excess adrenaline that your body releases in response to stress.

Get out of your own way! Don't set impossible tasks. Often we take too much on ourselves and blame ourselves for things we can do nothing about. It's important to focus on those things where you can make a difference. If you keep your head clear about the things you can do nothing about, then you may see clearly to find a way around them. If you're having a stressful day, take a few moments to think about what you can control and what you can't, and choose one or more tasks to focus on.

Make a personal play! Figure out specific strategies for stress reduction that work for you. If you can squeeze in a brisk thirty-minute walk or swim, it may clear away most of your stress. Or go to the movies, or write in your journal—whatever works for you. It may help to have a list of such activities to turn to when the stress heightens. The exercise strategy has two benefits. Activity burns a lot of the excess adrenaline that your body releases in response to stress. You can almost feel yourself calming down. The second benefit is that you are giving yourself a "time-out" from the stressful situation. When you ask regular exercisers why they exercise, 75 percent say that their major reason is stress reduction. Remember that you can walk just about anywhere—always have running or walking shoes with you!

More Strategies for Stress Management

Here are several additional useful strategies:

Biofeedback. In one simple study we asked people to sit quietly and focus on slowing their heart rate by looking at their heart rate on a wrist monitor. While they looked at the readout, they repeated very softly "down, down" or "slower, slower." Participants were not only able to lower their heart rate, but they also were able to lower their anxiety level and their blood pressure.

Simply using the rhythms of your body as a focus point can be a powerful stimulus to get you into the here and now. You don't need a heart rate monitor; you can take your pulse or focus on your breathing, a technique that works well for many. Sit quickly and focus your attention on your breathing. Clear your mind. Take slow, deep breaths in and out while paying very close attention to the breath pattern. If thoughts intrude, gently push them away and focus on breathing.

Tapping into mind/body connections. In another research experiment, we asked two groups of people to walk, but we asked

Seven Tips for Managing Stress

▲ Live in the present. Don't regret the past or fear the future.

▲ Always do your activity. Don't drop it when pressure mounts.

▲ Take a ten-minute timeout. Use a biofeedback or visualization technique to calm your thoughts.

▲ Stay flexible. There's usually more than one way to solve a problem.

▲ Anticipate. Plan ahead so that you are prepared.

▲ Take care of yourself. If you're dealing with stress, get your rest, cut back on caffeine, and take frequent short breaks.

▲ Seek support. Don't go it alone. Likewise, don't vent anger or hostility on those supporting you.

Seven Ways *Not* to Manage Stress

▲ Mindless eating

▲ Indulging in "comfort food" such as doughnuts or ice cream

▲ Vegging on the couch with dip and DVDs

▲ Driving fast

▲ Smoking

▲ Turning to alcohol

▲ Abusing drugs

one group to repeat a simple phrase to themselves while walking. For some this was a religious phrase or a philosophical phrase, or "left, right" as their left foot, then right foot touched down. Those who had a mental strategy achieved significantly more stress reduction than the people who simply walked. This technique may work for you.

Visualization. If you are in a stressful situation, visualizing yourself in a happier or more comfortable situation may help lower your stress level. Elite athletes, before a race or other competition, may close their eyes and become very still. What they are typically doing is visualizing their performance and lowering their stress level. You can combine this with slow breathing as well.

Further resources. You can find many good books, tapes, and programs for stress reduction. Two useful books that I strongly recommend, *Wherever You Go, You Are There: Mindfulness, Meditation and Everyday Life* and *Full Catastrophe Living: Using the Wisdom of Your Body and Mind to Face Stress, Pain and Illness,* were written by my friend and colleague, Dr. Jon Kabat-Zinn who ran the Mind/Body Stress Reduction Program at the University of Massachusetts Medical School. Dr. Kabat-Zinn has done some wonderful work showing how meditation techniques can substantially lower your stress and bring other benefits, such as pain relief.

Taking Time to Rest and Refresh

Many people confuse resting and relaxing with wasting time. Nothing could be further from the truth! Rest is a time when our bodies repair and our souls refresh. Rest is an active process where our bodies process things that have happened to us during the day and undergo a repair process right down to the level of every individual cell.

We live in a society that seems to be always busy. I understand the pressures to get things done. I manage a busy travel schedule, along with writing and consulting and seeing patients, and running a large clinic and research organization. It is imperative for me also to find time to be the best husband and father that I can be.

Does this sound familiar? I'll bet it does! The secret to doing what you want to with joy and satisfaction is not multitasking but being as disciplined as you can in setting priorities and making sure you have space to rest and relax each day.

Active Rest

Rest is a necessary process. It is not loafing or being lazy! Finding ways in our hectic stress-filled lives to truly rest and allow our bodies and souls to recover and repair themselves is vitally important. I believe it is virtually impossible to achieve balance in our lives unless we find time to allow health-promoting and rebalancing rest.

Active rest will mean different things to different people. My walking, running, or swimming sessions represent a critically important time of "active rest" where I think about problems from a different perspective and get into a different mindset and different environment. It is amazing to me how often problems will resolve during these periods of active rest. It's almost like magic! Because I am relaxing and letting my mind float freely, I've discovered new insights into issues that are best attacked indirectly.

Rest is a time when our bodies repair and our souls refresh.

Some people find the same quality of active rest through various hobbies or activities, such as gardening, playing a recreational sport, or participating in aerobic dance classes. Others may enjoy singing in an ensemble or chorus, playing in the community orchestra, or participating in community theater. Still others find great relaxation in sitting in an easy chair and reading a book or listening to their favorite tunes on their MP3 player. Rest can come in many different forms, but it is an active process that is absolutely essential for recalibrating and rebalancing both our bodies and our souls.

Relaxation

Relaxation is critically important, not only for emotional well-being but also for performing at our best. Before a presentation, if I make a concerted effort to relax, the presentation goes much smoother. Just like rest, relaxation is an active process. For most of us, it takes a concerted effort to calm ourselves down and to recognize when we are uptight and need to relax. My wife and I tell our children before a vocal concert or athletic event to take a deep breath and focus on relaxing their body. It may seem a disarmingly simple strategy, but recognizing when you need to stop what you are doing and spend a few minutes in relaxation can make an enormous difference.

Sleep

Sleep is a component of rest that may pose a very significant problem for many of us. Many studies have shown that most adults need seven or eight hours of sleep a night. Yet the average American gets less than seven hours of sleep on week nights and many survive on far fewer. If you are sleeping less than five hours a night or more than nine hours a night, realize that these habits may be associated with poor health.

Rest gives our bodies time to decrease the stresses on some of the systems and focus energy on the repair processes necessary for healing.

One of every three adults suffers from some sleep problems occasionally, and more than 70 million people have some level of sleep problem.[7] This is part of what has driven an upsurge in sales of pharmaceutical therapies for sleep. I see far too many people who have been given a sleep medication before their physician has really delved into issues in their daily lifestyle, which may enhance sleep better than pharmaceutical therapy.

Four components of what the researchers called "sleep hygiene" may make an enormous difference in your ability to get to sleep and the quality of sleep:

▲ Use your bedroom for sleep and not for other activities such as watching television, eating, or playing loud music.

▲ Go to bed and get up at the same time every day.

▲ Avoid exercise or alcohol late at night; get regular activity during the day; try a hot bath before bedtime.

▲ Learn progressive relaxation techniques, such as focusing on your breathing or progressively relaxing various parts of your muscles from toes on up to your head.

If these suggestions don't work and you are still having trouble sleeping, try cognitive therapy with a behavioral specialist or psychologist. A good night's sleep is important to a balanced lifestyle.

Repair

People with serious illnesses are put on bed rest for a reason. There is also a reason we feel the need to sleep more and rest when we have a bad cold. Rest gives our bodies time to decrease the stresses on some of the systems and to focus energy on the repair processes necessary for healing. In fact, this repair occurs even at the cellular level. It has been estimated that, as part of normal metabolism and the outside environment, every cell in our bodies daily experiences between one thousand and one million molecular "lesions" or damage that require repair. Active rest lets the cell focus energy on making the repairs necessary to sustain the very life of the cell. These cells, remember, make up all the systems of our bodies. Adequate rest promotes the body's physical repair, a vital part of health and well-being.

We would all benefit if we could spend at least one half a day every week in a retreat that allows us to regenerate both physically and mentally.

Retreat

In addition to active rest, we need times when we can retreat from the world. This may be the time you take for yourself, as we discussed in the previous section, or it may be time you spend with family or friends. Retreat may be as simple as a few moments of quiet meditation or something as elaborate as a spiritual retreat that lasts for a few days or longer.

Many religions incorporate the idea of retreat into their concept of the Sabbath or a day of rest. Unfortunately, many of us now use a "day of rest" as a time for frenetic activity to do those things that we couldn't get done on the other days. I think this is a mistake. We would all benefit if we could spend at least half a day every week in a retreat that allows us to regenerate both physically and mentally.

My family finds that the best, most relaxing vacations are family retreats in the country where we just enjoy each other's company. Find vacation strategies that allow you to retreat and relax—not vacations that leave you worn out!

Active Recovery

The concept of "active recovery" comes from sports and athletics. You may have seen that, following a race, athletes may jog for a few minutes or walk to cool down. This allows their bodies to process some of the waste products that developed during a vigorous athletic event. We could take a lesson from these athletes and recognize that in our daily lives, we need to practice active rest and recovery to help manage the stresses and strains that we confront. In a sense, these periods of active recovery, whether they be rest, sleep, or retreats, help us free our bodies of toxic physical and mental stresses. Active rest and recovery help us stay in balance.

Eight Keys to Emotional Well-Being

Establishing emotional well-being is an important component of achieving overall well-being and balance. Many of us spend considerable time and energy trying to figure out what emotional well-being is all about. Negative emotions such as anger, fear, or resentment get in the way of our emotional well-being. Here are eight opportunities to improve emotional well-being:

1. Passion and commitment

We all know people who live their lives with great passion and intensity. This ability to engage fully and with deep commitment in life is, in my view, one of the prerequisites for emotional well-being. Passion and commitment require a purpose. What purposes or goals engage you passionately? What fully engages your enthusiasm, your mind, your efforts? When you answer these questions, if only partially, you will possess an important key to well-being.

2. Love and intimacy

Many poets and philosophers have written beautifully about the importance of love in emotional well-being. In his moving and inspiring book, *Man's Search for Meaning*, Viktor Frankl states, "Love is the ultimate and highest goal to which a man can aspire."[8] He goes on to say, "The salvation of man is through love and in love." I believe that finding love and building intimacy are essential to the emotional well-being and meaning that we all seek. This deep love springs from the core of the soul. I encourage you to focus great energy and commitment on those people around you to establish the love and intimacy that is essential for emotional well-being.

3. Living intentionally

We always tell our patients and research participants that we

127

are not asking them to turn their lives upside down, just to live more intentionally. Examine your life and look for the opportunities to find joy and happiness, as well as meaning and well-being.

4. Discipline and focus

Living intentionally requires discipline. By adding structure to our lives, we create the kind of space that allows us to explore various emotions and interact with people around us. Living intentionally also allows us to focus our energy on those things that are important and discard those things that are less important. If you focus your energies intentionally on trying to achieve balance and well-being in your life, it will make an enormous difference in your ability to reach your goals.

5. Self-acceptance and affirmation

True emotional well-being may be elusive until you accept yourself. This key quality may seem obvious, but many of us struggle with it. Accepting that you are worthy of having a more joyful, meaningful life is essential. Eleanor Roosevelt, who overcame self-doubts to lead a remarkable life of service for human welfare, once said, "No one can make you feel inferior without your consent." Remember that and quit giving yourself consent to go on thinking you are not worth the effort.

6. Spirituality

Connecting with our spiritual side is one of the important ways that we connect with our inner most being, as well as with other human beings. Unfortunately, many of us neglect our spiritual health. Seeking to find and explore and practice what brings deepest meaning to your life can help ground you even in the midst of pain and trauma.

7. Forgiveness

Forgiveness may be very difficult, particularly if others have wronged us or insulted us, but it is critical to restoring relationships and achieving personal well-being. We also must forgive ourselves for past bonds or perceived shortcomings. In *The Return of the Prodigal Son*, the theologian Henri Nouwen makes the point that there is no room for resentment in a heart that is able to forgive.[9] Resentment is crippling, corrosive, and self-limiting. But forgiveness, as Nouwen says, carries the important element of compassion. Compassion for others and for ourselves benefits us greatly if we can find the strength to forgive, both ourselves and others.

8. Embracing joy

Many of us spend a great deal of time looking for ways to be happier in our lives. However, far fewer of us spend time in pursuing the deeper quality that I call "joy." It is easy to get so caught up in planning for the future that you neglect to appreciate all the things that are happening now. All of us could benefit from looking for those wonderful things that happen each day in our lives that provide the basis for true joy. Embracing this wonderful aspect of our human existence helps affirm emotional well-being.

Two Lifestyle Issues that Affect Well-Being

In the Balanced Life Index, we included two issues that affect balance and well-being for many people. Being overweight or obese is a complex issue that is entwined in many aspects of health and balance, including nutrition, activity, and particular issues of well-being. Smoking also poses risks to balance in health and well-being.

Weight Management and Well-Being

Maintaining your weight within a healthy range (BMI 18.6 to 24.9) provides many benefits. You significantly lower your risk of heart disease, diabetes, stroke, high blood pressure, arthritis, and some cancers. You're less likely to experience depression and anxiety. You look and feel your best. And you'll likely live longer.

Keeping your weight balanced can be a challenge. About two-thirds of American adults are overweight or obese (BMI 25 and over).[10] Being underweight (BMI 18.4 and under) increases your health risks. From 0.7 to 2.4 percent of American adults are underweight.[11]

The recommendations of MyPyramid and the strategies of *Your Plan for a Balanced Life* can help you maintain a healthy weight or lose or gain weight. Here are some tips:

Strategies for Losing Weight—Keeping It Simple

1. Burn more calories than you eat. Reducing your daily caloric intake by about five hundred calories typically results in losing one to two pounds weekly, which is a healthy rate. Emphasize nutrient-dense foods, not discretionary calories, while following the Balanced Nutrition Plan. The Meal Planner on StartMakingChoices.com can create menus to help you achieve this goal.

Research shows that the most successful long-term weight loss and maintenance strategies combine balanced nutrition with regular activity.

2. Get regular physical activity. Regular physical activity (thirty minutes a day) helps maintain lean muscle mass and metabolism while you lose weight. Research shows that the most successful, long-term weight loss and maintenance strategies combine balanced nutrition with regular activity.

3. Think long-term balance, not short-term diet. People who lose weight and keep it off long-term adopt balanced nutritional and activity strategies as a new way of living, not as a short-term diet.

Strategies for Gaining Weight—Keeping It Simple

If you are underweight, the strategies of balanced nutrition and activity will help alleviate this condition. Consulting a nutrition or healthcare professional is also wise. Adults who may be at risk for anorexia or bulimia should consult a healthcare professional.

1. Eat more calories than you burn. Increasing your daily caloric intake by one hundred to five hundred calories will promote weight gain. Use the MyPyramid recommendations to select foods that are nutrient- and energy-dense. Consider nutritionally balanced supplements for snacks or with a meal. Use the Meal Planner on StartMakingChoices.com to plan menus that meet your calorie and nutrition goals.

2. Get regular physical activity. Activities like light walking, light strength training, and stretching will help you stay fit while gaining weight.

Smoking and Well-Being

Smoking is a habit that affects your quality of life and well-being. It's the leading cause of preventable death in the U.S., contributing to more than four hundred thousand deaths annually. Secondhand smoke increases bronchitis in children who live with a smoker and poses other risks. Smoking is a barrier to achieving optimal balance in life.

Most smokers know the dangers of smoking, and most want to quit. If you smoke, quitting should be one of your goals for balanced well-being. But quitting isn't easy. It may take many tries. A wide range of support, from medication to structured cessation programs, is available. Helpful Web sites include the American Heart Association (www.americanheart.org), the American Cancer Society (www.cancer.org), the National Cancer Institute (www.nci.nih.gov), and the American Lung Association (www.lungusa.org). *The Last Puff*, by John Farquhar and Gene Spiller, describes techniques many former smokers have used to quit.[12]

Making It Real: Betsy's Story

Betsy, 46, had risen to vice president of marketing for a large company but felt that her work life was eroding her family and personal time. While she enjoyed her success at work, she knew her husband and two teenage daughters shared her concern. She wanted to get her life back in balance.

Not surprisingly, her initial BLI score for well-being was low. She was very dissatisfied with the time she had for herself and her family, because work demands and a constant barrage of e-mail interrupted every evening. She felt major stress, and although she knew she shouldn't smoke, cigarettes alleviated some of her stress and helped her maintain a stable weight. She was not surprised that her well-being score on her BLI was 100 (out of 300), which placed her in the lowest category.

Motivated to make some changes, Betsy gradually implemented her change strategies over the next six months. She made a daily "appointment" in her planner of fifteen to twenty minutes of uninterrupted private time. To better balance work and home life, she began checking business e-mail only once each evening, after dinner, and she only responded to emergencies. Setting this simple boundary lowered her stress and increased her time with her family.

As a next step, Betsy gradually cut back to smoking less than half a pack per day, and she enrolled in a quit smoking support group. Six months later, Betsy had quit smoking entirely and was walking four times weekly, using the Balanced Walking Program. Her success in adopting small strategies to improve her well-being has given Betsy new confidence and happiness in life.

Personalizing Your Well-Being Plan

It's time to create some priorities for your balanced well-being plan. Look at the goal-setting worksheet at the end of this chapter and write down one well-being goal that you feel is most important to work on. Develop some specific strategies and action steps for it. Then prioritize your other goals and write down strategies and action steps for them as well.

Don't forget that the journey toward balance is sometimes made easier when you take the journey with a friend. StartMakingChoices.com offers a virtual community of experts (including me) and people just like you who are trying to find balance. The Well-Being portion of the site will regularly feature new articles on  stress relief, work/life balance, and other well-being topics. You can also follow other people's progress as they post to their blogs. As the community grows, you may even find yourself becoming a trusted expert to someone else.

As you are planning, remember that well-being covers many personal concerns and issues related to balance. So think carefully about how the various goals, strategies, and action steps you've identified fit together. Onward to success!

Your Plan for a Balanced Life
Goal-Setting Worksheet: Well-Being

Goal 1: _____

    Strategy: _____

        Action Steps: _____

    Strategy: _____

        Action Steps: _____

    Strategy: _____

        Action Steps: _____

Goal 2: _____

    Strategy: _____

        Action Steps: _____

    Strategy: _____

        Action Steps: _____

    Strategy: _____

        Action Steps: _____

Goal 3: _____

    Strategy: _____

        Action Steps: _____

    Strategy: _____

        Action Steps: _____

    Strategy: _____

        Action Steps: _____

Activating Your Personal Plan to Achieve a Balanced Life

The big moment has arrived. It's time to pull all your ideas into a simple, organized plan that will help you achieve more balance in your life. You may remember that there are four steps that will take you from wishing for changes to actually making them:

1. Assess your specific needs. Your scores on the Balanced Life Index indicated areas where you are strong and where you need to work. You prioritized some major goals based on the BLI and your wishes.

2. Make a practical plan that addresses your needs. With your prioritized major goals in mind, you used the goal-setting worksheets to identify specific, measurable goals and strategies and action steps to help you achieve those goals. In a moment, you are going to turn those goals and strategies into a Program Calendar.

3. View your plan as ongoing and long-term. The goal is to make positive changes that help you live in a balanced way. You determine the action steps in your plan, and you set the pace. For motivation, you can keep track of progress using the tracker that's part of your Program Calendar, or the online plan and tracker at

StartMakingChoices.com. Reassess, affirm, and adjust at intervals to keep going forward.

4. Establish a support team. If you have a family, invite them to participate with you, support you, and be your "team." If you are single and do not have children, reach out to friends. Share the ideas for a balanced life. You might recruit a team who likes to do it with you or at least cheer you on.

Putting Your Personal Plan Together

Because the three domains of balance—nutrition, activity, and well-being—work together, you selected one major priority goal in each domain from your list of goals. These power your plan. You then used goal-setting worksheets to identify specific goals and make notes about strategies and action steps as you read the chapters on nutrition, activity, and well-being.

Let's put them all together. You have three options:

1. You can use our blank form for the Balanced Program Calendar and Tracker on page 141 and tailor your program from scratch.

2. You can skip to page 142 and use our Balanced Program Calendar and Tracker template as your base and modify it.

3. You can use the customized program on StartMarkingChoices.com. Signing up is quick, easy, and free. Based on your information and BLI score, a Weekly Plan with recommended meal and activity options is generated for you. You can customize the recommended options with your favorite meals and activities.  StartMakingChoices.com will store all of your information, making it easy to log and track your individual choices against the recommended plan. You can even print off your plan for reference, and you can track yourself online. (Remember not to start everything at once, particularly aerobic and strength training.)

Plan Your Own Program from Scratch

First, we'll look at a sample of what to do, then I'll give you a form to get started. Let's assume that your first priority goal to balance nutrition is to consume at least the daily recommended servings of fruit. You've also decided to get started on the Balanced Walking Program and just generally try to be more active. For well-being, your primary goal is more time with family and friends. You've decided to make time for them and based your action steps on that strategy.

A sample of what your calendar might look like for weeks one and two is on page 140. As you see, you can fill in as much or as little as works for you. Also note that it's a good idea to put down when you plan to use the Balanced Life Index to check your progress.

As your action steps turn into healthy new habits, continue to add new goals and strategies to your planner. My recommendation is that you plan about a month in advance and update just once a month. Of course, whatever works for you is fine—weekly, bi-weekly, bi-monthly. Remember to be flexible. Your plan is a guide—it's not carved in stone. It simply helps keep you on track.

Plan Your Program Using the Template

If you'd like a little structure or a sample, a program calendar template is on page 142. It includes the walking program because it's easy to launch while you get ready to try the two-week meal plan. You may reverse these if you like. Feel free to modify strategies and action steps to fit your needs. Be flexible.

To help you in your continuing assessment and planning process, you'll find a complete set of planning tools in the appendix. Feel free to copy them.

Balanced Program Calendar and Tracker

S=Strategy; A=Action Step   Check to track action

Week #1		Strategies and Action Steps	M	T	W	T	F	S	S
Nutrition	S	Eat at least 5 more servings of fruit this week							
	A	Take fruit for afternoon snack MWF							
	A	Fruit for dessert after 2 dinners							
Activity	S & A	Carry out Walking Program Week 1							
	A	Use steps at work when possible							
Well-Being	A	Sat afternoon: family hike and picnic at state park							
Week #2									
Nutrition	S & A	Continue strategy of snacks & desserts from Week 1							
	A	Add fruit to breakfast Tuesday, Thursday, and Saturday to total eight additional servings							
Activity	S & A	Carry out Walking Program Week 2							
Well-Being	A	Thursday: ask neighbors over to grill out							
End of WK 2		Retake BLI for progress check							

Balanced Program Calendar and Tracker								
Week	Strategies and Action Steps	M	T	W	T	F	S	S

Balanced Program Calendar and Tracker TEMPLATE									
Week		Strategies and Action Steps	M	T	W	T	F	S	S
Week 1									
Activity		Start Walking Program Week 1							
Nutrition		Eat at least 1 vegetable (other than potato) at lunch and dinner every day							
Well-Being		Stress management priority: Walking program							
Week 2									
Activity		Walking Program Week 2							
Nutrition		Continue veggie action step							
		Read two-week meal plan; make shopping list							
Well-Being		Stress management: Use 10-minute time-out at work							
ASSESS		Retake BLI and note progress							
Week 3									
Activity		Walking Program Week 3 Take the stairs at work							
Nutrition		Continue veggie strategy; add fruit for snack							
		Shop for two-week meal plan							
Well-Being		Select family time strategy							
Week 4									
Activity		Walking Program Week 4							
Nutrition		Start meal plan week 1							
Well-Being		Continue intentional family time							
ASSESS		Retake BLI and note progress Reward!!!							
Week 5									
Activity		Walking Program Week 5							
Nutrition		Continue meal plan week 2							
Well-Being		Plan half day for self							
Week 6									
Activity		Walking Program Week 6							
Nutrition		Use meal planner to plan this week's meals; repeat meals from two-week plan that we enjoyed; select own favorites that emphasize veggie goals							
Well-Being		Family outing: hike, picnic, show, ballgame							
ASSESS		Retake BLI and note progress							
Week 7		Continue in this course							

Plan Your Program Using the Planner and Tools at StartMakingChoices.com

You can expand your experience with *Your Plan for a Balanced Life* at StartMakingChoices.com. After you sign up, you have access to all the online tools that help you manage and track the three fundamentals of the plan: nutrition, activity, and well-being. Membership is free and signing up only takes a few minutes.

Creating Your Plan for a Balanced Life

After you complete the survey and receive your BLI, you will receive a starter plan that's customized to your food, activity, and well-being preferences. You can fine-tune your plan by identifying your personal goals for balance, your favorite foods, and your desired activities.

Tracking Your Progress

Log your daily activities to see how many calories you've burned and how active you've been. Enter what you've eaten to keep track of your nutrition plan. The personal log will update your BLI automatically. The more frequently you use the logs, the more useful and accurate your progress tracking will be. A variety of charts, graphs, and trackers show how well you are meeting your goals over time. It's easy to check your progress to ensure that you are maximizing your potential.

Although your BLI score is personal to you, you can also see how your score stacks up with other StartMakingChoices.com members— for a little motivation.

Accessing Support for Success

StartMakingChoices.com provides many tools and features you can use. Many experts provide helpful tips, advice, and coaching to the membership community. Frequent posting of new articles, tips, recipes, and tools provides information that is seasonal, helpful, and personal.

If you enjoy cooking, you'll really enjoy the robust recipes and meal planning tools. You can search for recipes by a variety of categories including cooking time and ingredients or try recommended seasonal favorites.

Use a variety of tools and educational resources to stay informed and help you make smarter decisions: calculators to determine your BMI, target heart rate for cardio activity, optimal calorie intake, and a nutrition label guide to help you better understand how to read nutrition labels are just a few of the tools that are available.

Sharing Community

Achieving your goals can be easier when you share the journey with a friend. StartMakingChoices.com offers

a growing set of community features that let you share stories and advice and ask for feedback and help. Message boards allow you to connect with others in the StartMakingChoices.com

A Note about Weight Problems

If one of your goals is to work toward a healthy weight—whether you need to gain or lose—the steps for change in *Your Plan for a Balanced Life* are ideal. With its emphasis on balanced nutrition, adequate activity, and attention to well-being issues, your plan can easily be tailored to help you meet your weight goals. Remember that a healthy, safe goal for weight loss is one to two pounds a week. Higher losses are associated not only with loss of fluids but with loss of lean muscle mass, which is counter-productive. If your goal is to lose fat, make sure to maintain lean muscle mass, the body's metabolism engine. So your plan should include both nutrition and regular physical activity.

Here are several tips to help you modify your plan to meet weight goals:

Nutrition for weight loss. The key to losing weight is to consume less energy (calories) than you expend in the activities of daily life and in any activity. As a rule of thumb, your eating plan for weight loss should have about 500 calories fewer than the amount you need to maintain your weight. For example, if you maintain your weight by eating 2,100 calories a day, then you would aim to consume 1,600 calories for weight loss. Be aware that eating less than 1,200 calories a day is strongly discouraged because it is difficult to fit in adequate nutrients—and may cause your body to go into "starvation" mode and actually slow down metabolism. In making meal plans, continue to follow your goals for balanced nutrition, emphasizing plenty of fruits and vegetables, lowered fat intakes, and lean protein. Signing up for the online program at StartMakingChoices. com can help you to make meal plans for your target calorie level for weight management and to chart your progress.

Nutrition for weight gain. If you need to gain weight, you would aim for 500 more calories than needed to maintain your current weight. If 1,600 daily calories would maintain your current weight, aim at 2,100 daily calories. Emphasize foods that offer both nutrients and calories.

Physical activity. To preserve lean muscle mass and to help with fat loss, you need to get regular aerobic activity. The Balanced Walking Plan is ideal. Just keep moving. If you want to gain weight, you'll still want to do an exercise program for all its health benefits.

Well-being. Stress can often sabotage your plans for weight change. Using some of our tips for stress management can help you avoid pitfalls such as mindless eating or letting your activity program lapse, or losing your appetite and skipping meals.

Consistency does it. Everyone is going to fall off their plan sometimes. Don't use a short-term lapse or missing a day of exercise as an excuse to quit. Live in the present. Pick up where you left off. If you've slipped back a little further, then reach back and start at a point that fits. There will be peaks and valleys. Long-term consistency brings you to your goals.

community; you may even make a few friends. A monthly e-mail newsletter provides seasonally relevant and personalized tips, recipes, advice, and offers.

It's That Easy

When you've done your homework—assessing your needs and prioritizing goals— the actual planning is a breeze. In the next chapter, we'll explore some common challenges that you might encounter as you implement your plan.

Getting on Track—and Staying There

Over the past twenty-five years as a physician and a researcher, I have seen thousands of people succeed in making changes in their lives, and I have seen many falter. Here's what I have concluded: People falter on the practical issues—which are easy to resolve if you have strategies in place.

Six Paths to Success

Over the years, we have identified six main barriers that get in the way of improving balance in your life.

1. Kick the procrastination habit.

We all do it. We may think, *Tomorrow I will start my walking program* or *Tomorrow I will start eating more fruits and vegetables since I'm too tired to go to the grocery store today* or *Tomorrow, I'll call our friends about coming over for dinner*

147

sometime. We all find ways to put off those things that we not only ought to do but also genuinely want to do. Inertia is a powerful physical and emotional force; perhaps we fear failure. The best way to break through the procrastination barrier is to identify it. Then take the time to take one small step *today* rather than tomorrow. Maybe that step is a ten-minute walk or calling a friend. Taking small steps regularly will take a little planning and preparation. But if you've read this far, you've already begun.

2. Make realistic goals.

We have all known people who tried to lose ten pounds the week before their high school or college reunion or just in time for bathing suit season. While it may be possible to lose ten pounds of water in a week, it is very unhealthy, and inevitably this weight comes back. Over and over, people make serious errors when it comes to changing their life by framing the issues incorrectly and pursuing fundamentally flawed strategies from day one.

Over and over, people make serious errors when it comes to changing their lives by framing the issues incorrectly.

Volunteers for our walking studies often think running would be more effective than walking, but many of them have been sedentary for years. Running would not only be very uncomfortable, but would also endanger their bones and joints.

As you think about changing your life and improving its balance, ask yourself:

1. *What do I want to change to improve balance in my life?*
2. *What would fit within the realities of my life so that I can do it without turning my life upside down?*

By assessing your current status and thinking about where you wish to change, you are framing plans for change that are likely to succeed.

3. Tap into your personal power.

Many of us don't believe deep down that we have the power within ourselves to make positive changes in our life. We tend to look at the times we've fallen short of our goals rather than the times we've succeeded. Often it seems that circumstances are against us. In psychology, "locus of control" describes where each person feels the power to make changes resides. Those people who have an inner locus of control believe that they have the power to take the steps to make changes in their lives. Those people who have an "external" locus of control believe that they are essentially powerless and that

> *Those people who have an inner locus of control believe that they have the power to take the steps to make changes in their lives.*

their life's course is determined by others. Think carefully about your attitudes about control. Are you giving away your power? You do have the ability to achieve balance and change in your life. If you feel stuck, perhaps you're not framing the issues properly. Can you walk ten minutes today or tomorrow? Can you make your lunch on whole-grain bread? If you can do these small steps, you are on your way.

4. Think positively.

Sometimes we feel that we have to achieve all our dreams and goals or we have failed. Volunteers in our weight management studies may say, "But I'll never be able to lose the target goal I want; I've never been able to before." The danger of this approach is that if you don't achieve your goal, you feel you are a complete failure and give up. Often the target goal these people have in mind is not even realistic. I've seen volunteers in our weight management studies lose thirty pounds in thirty weeks and feel they were failures because they didn't lose fifty! A pound a week weight loss is a very realistic and healthy level.

Recognize that the process of change will have peaks and valleys and that sticking with the program at some times will be easier than at other times. Give yourself credit for the positives you achieve, not blame for the possibly pie-in-the-sky goal you didn't quite make. Build on your achievements realistically, and you may surprise yourself by one day surpassing that pie-in-the-sky goal.

5. Plan ahead.

Often people who have excellent intentions falter on basic issues related to planning and preparation. You may jeopardize your walking program if you fail to plan where you will walk or what you will do when the weather is too hot, too cold, too snowy, too rainy, too whatever! Many people would like to eat more fruits and vegetables but don't take steps to make it easier. If you leave apples and bananas in a fruit bowl in the kitchen and keep cut-up carrots and celery in a container within easy reach in the fridge, you're far more likely to eat them. The list goes on: Failing to write your daily activity sessions in your planner makes it easier to skip; failing to set consistent goals means you probably won't adopt any coordinated, effective changes long-term. Again, most people falter on small issues, not cosmic ones, when it comes to making positive changes to achieve balance. Planning and preparation may seem like simple steps, but they are absolutely critical to achieving your goal.

Planning and preparation are critical to achieving your goal.

6. Live in the present.

Most of us spend too much time either regretting the past or fearing the future. Seek strategies that will allow you to live in the moment. Yes, planning and preparation are important, but the goal of planning is to free you up to live in the present, to let go the past (you can't change it), and not to fear the future (you've planned for it and you're prepared to be flexible).

Mastering the Hurdles, Winning the Race

Undertaking a plan to make changes to improve balance in your life is like a hurdle race. Of course, you can see the finish line, but to get there, you have to jump over a bunch of hurdles. Many people make the mistake of looking only at the finish line and don't keep an eye out for each hurdle in front of them. If you can keep your focus on both the steps you're taking and the hurdles—the practical issues that can get in your way— you can pace yourself to victory, achieving your goal of improved balance, permanent change, and a healthier, happier lifestyle.

Making It Real: Susan and Mark

In their early thirties, Susan and Mark have twin 3-year-old boys and a 6-month-old daughter. Like many two-career couples with young children, they felt every day teetered on the edge of chaos. They wanted to get back in balance. When they took the Balanced Life survey they scored near the bottom on both nutrition and activity but had good well-being scores. Susan and Mark discovered that their nutrition was out of balance. Both ate only a $\frac{1}{2}$ cup of fruits and vegetables daily. Fast food lunches often featured cheeseburgers or burritos with sodas. Susan and Mark knew they ate too many empty-calorie sweets and snacks. Together they planned some gradual changes in their nutritional habits. They wanted to eat better for themselves, but more important, they wanted to set a better example for their children.

Over the next three months, Susan and Mark gradually increased the fruits and vegetables they ate. Using the meal planner, they made sure they had ingredients for a salad and vegetable as part of dinner. To increase whole grains, they made lunch sandwiches on whole-grain bread and included more whole-grain pastas at dinner. They also took a carton of milk or 100% juice to go with lunch. They began reserving their consumption of sweets for dessert after dinner, and for crunchy treats, they chose popcorn, carrot, and celery sticks over fried potato chips. With these simple changes, their BLI nutrition score moved into the excellent category. The most impressive thing about the Balanced Nutrition Program, Susan said, was how big an impact a few simple choices made.

> *Remember that balance is about gradually adopting changes to arrive at a new way of living that makes you healthier and happier.*

Encouraged by this success, Susan and Mark started walking during their lunch breaks, following the Balanced Walking Program. On weekends, they planned to walk with the children. The pace would be slower but everyone could enjoy the time together. "Our life is just as busy," said Mark, "but now we feel in charge. Using the plan helped us make the choices that we needed to reach our goals."

Getting Back on Track

Who doesn't slip out of balance? Remember that failure is not falling down, it's staying down.

Relapse isn't collapse. Don't fall into the trap of using a slipup—whether indulging in holiday treats or failing to walk for a week—as a reason to quit. If an inner voice is saying to you *Oh, you can't stick* *with anything*, answer back and say, *Oh, yes, I can, and I'm going to prove it!* Don't waste time regretting what you've done—move on! What can you do right this minute to start getting back in balance? Maybe you can put this book down and walk around the block or just around the house. Or you can reach for an apple, do some toe raises, or plan a healthy dinner. Every small step forward helps!

Analyze why you slipped. Were your goals realistic? How can you reframe them to make them more practical? Did you try to do too much at once—such as completely change how you eat and begin a walking program? Remember that balance is about gradually adopting changes to arrive at a new way of living that makes you healthier and happier. You pick the goals and you set the pace that works for you.

Did physical issues arise? If a painful knee or heel spur kept you from walking, look for a water aerobics class you can attend. Or work with a physical therapist to resolve the physical problem. For every problem, there's a solution.

Remember that you're worth it. Remind yourself that you are worthy of the effort—even if you don't believe it at the moment. Remind yourself to live in the present, to look at what you wish to do today and to quit dwelling on the past. Then take just one positive step today to head in the direction you desire.

Don't forget to laugh and enjoy the little pleasures of today.

Move forward. To get out of any uncomfortable place we find ourselves in, we have to move forward, to move on. We don't really want to go in circles. We need to look at what's in our way, understand those blocks, and move through them. The simple planning strategies in this book can help you refocus and adapt your choices so that you move through.

Celebrate your accomplishments. You have done something positive even if all you have done is start making a plan as you read this book. Look at what you have done. Most people have come much farther than they give themselves credit for. Celebrate those accomplishments. Remember to frame the issues properly.

Laugh every day. A little humor can lighten your spirits and help put things in perspective. We often take small mishaps too seriously. And slipping away from your goals can be just a small mishap. Much depends on your perspective. Think positively. Focus on what you can do, not what you *didn't* do. And don't forget to laugh and enjoy the little pleasures of today.

Keeping the momentum. We're all human. There will be times when you don't follow your plan perfectly. The important thing is to focus on the overall changes you are making and not let a one-time slip cause you to give up completely. Instead of dwelling on a missed exercise class or a high-calorie treat, focus on the successes you have achieved. If you feel your motivation fading, refresh your strategies by retaking the Balanced Life Index and using the goal-setting worksheets for nutrition, activity, and well-being. Repeat the two-week meal plan; re-launch the walking program. And reward yourself for the effort and courage to continue seeking balance.

Appendix A
Planning Tools

Go to StartMakingChoices.com for easy-to-use interactive worksheets.

Balanced Life Index Record of My Scores

Date of Score	Total Score	Nutrition	Activity	Well-Being

Goal-Setting Worksheet

Goal 1: _____

   Strategy: _____

      Action Steps: _____

   Strategy: _____

      Action Steps: _____

   Strategy: _____

      Action Steps: _____

Goal 2: _____

   Strategy: _____

      Action Steps: _____

   Strategy: _____

      Action Steps: _____

   Strategy: _____

      Action Steps: _____

Goal 3: _____

   Strategy: _____

      Action Steps: _____

   Strategy: _____

      Action Steps: _____

   Strategy: _____

      Action Steps: _____

Balanced Program Tracker and Calendar

Week	S/A	Strategies and Action Steps	M	T	W	T	F	S	S

Food Diary Checklist

Use this checklist to keep a simple diary of what you eat each day. Use one sheet per day. This checklist is based on a 2,000 calorie diet; your needs might vary. Refer to the MyPyramid Food Pattern table below to determine the daily recommended amounts for each food group at your calorie level.

List all foods you ate today	Organize foods into MyPyramid Food Groups	MyPyramid Food Groups	Goals for a 2,000 calorie diet	Estimate your total
Breakfast		**Grains** At least half of the grains you consume should be whole grains.	**6 ounce equivalents** (Ex. 1 oz.: 1 slice bread, 1 mini bagel, 1 small muffin, ½ cup oatmeal, 3 cups popcorn, 1 cup cereal flakes or rounds, ½ cup rice, 1 small tortilla.)	☐☐☐ ☐☐☐ ounce equivalents
Lunch		**Vegetables** Try to eat a variety of vegetables every day.	**2¹/₂ cups** (Ex. 1 cup: 1 cup cooked or raw tomatoes, broccoli, corn, beans, peas; 1 medium baked potato, 1 cup pinto beans, or 2 cups raw leafy greens.)	☐☐◺ cups
Dinner		**Fruit** Choose whole fruit more often than fruit juice.	**2 cups** (Ex. 1 cup: 1 small apple, 1 large banana, 32 grapes, 1 large orange, 1 medium pear, 1 small peach, ½ cup raisins.)	☐☐ cups
		Milk Choose low-fat or fat-free milk.	**3 cups** (Ex. 1 cup: 1 cup milk, yogurt, pudding, frozen yogurt; 1½ oz. cheese, 2 oz. American cheese, ¹/₃ cup shredded cheese.)	☐☐☐ cups
Snack		**Meat and Beans** Choose lean meat and poultry. Vary your choices—add fish, nuts, and seeds.	**5¹/₂ ounce equivalents** (Ex. 1 oz.: 1 oz. cooked meat, poultry, or fish; 1 egg, 1 T peanut butter, ½ oz. sunflower seeds, ¼ cup cooked dry beans, 2 T hummus.)	☐☐☐ ☐☐◺ ounce equivalents

MyPyramid Food Patterns

Daily Amount of Food from Each Group

Calorie Level*	1,000	1,200	1,400	1,600	1,800	2,000	2,200	2,400	2,600	2,800	3,000	3,200
Fruits	1 cup	1 cup	1.5 cups	1.5 cups	1.5 cups	2 cups	2 cups	2 cups	2 cups	2.5 cups	2.5 cups	2.5 cups
Vegetables	1 cup	1.5 cups	1.5 cups	2 cups	2.5 cups	2.5 cups	3 cups	3 cups	3.5 cups	3.5 cups	4 cups	4 cups
Grains	3 ounce equivalents	4 ounce equivalents	5 ounce equivalents	5 ounce equivalents	6 ounce equivalents	6 ounce equivalents	7 ounce equivalents	8 ounce equivalents	9 ounce equivalents	10 ounce equivalents	10 ounce equivalents	10 ounce equivalents
Lean meat & beans	2 ounce equivalents	3 ounce equivalents	4 ounce equivalents	5 ounce equivalents	5 ounce equivalents	5.5 ounce equivalents	6 ounce equivalents	6.5 ounce equivalents	6.5 ounce equivalents	7 ounce equivalents	7 ounce equivalents	7 ounce equivalents
Milk	2 cups	2 cups	2 cups	3 cups	3 cups	3 cups	3 cups	3 cups	3 cups	3 cups	3 cups	3 cups
Discretionary	165	171	171	182	195	267	290	362	410	426	512	648

*To determine your calorie level, look at the Suggested Energy Intake Level chart on page 164.

Appendix B
Nutrition Tools

**Go to StartMakingChoices.com for a
web-based customized plan.**

Suggested Energy Intake (Calorie) Levels by Age, Gender, and Activity Level

	MALES				FEMALES		
Activity level	Sedentary*	Mod. active*	Active*	**Activity level**	Sedentary*	Mod. active*	Active*
AGE				**AGE**			
2	1000	1000	1000	2	1000	1000	1000
3	1000	1400	1400	3	1000	1200	1400
4	1200	1400	1600	4	1200	1400	1400
5	1200	1400	1600	5	1200	1400	1600
6	1400	1600	1800	6	1200	1400	1600
7	1400	1600	1800	7	1200	1600	1800
8	1400	1600	2000	8	1400	1600	1800
9	1600	1800	2000	9	1400	1600	1800
10	1600	1800	2200	10	1400	1800	2000
11	1800	2000	2200	11	1600	1800	2000
12	1800	2200	2400	12	1600	2000	2200
13	2000	2200	2600	13	1600	2000	2200
14	2000	2400	2800	14	1800	2000	2400
15	2200	2600	3000	15	1800	2000	2400
16	2400	2800	3200	16	1800	2000	2400
17	2400	2800	3200	17	1800	2000	2400
18	2400	2800	3200	18	1800	2000	2400
19-20	2600	2800	3000	19-20	2000	2200	2400
21-25	2400	2800	3000	21-25	2000	2200	2400
26-30	2400	2600	3000	26-30	1800	2000	2400
31-35	2400	2600	3000	31-35	1800	2000	2200
36-40	2400	2600	2800	36-40	1800	2000	2200
41-45	2200	2600	2800	41-45	1800	2000	2200
46-50	2200	2400	2800	46-50	1800	2000	2200
51-55	2200	2400	2800	51-55	1600	1800	2200
56-60	2200	2400	2600	56-60	1600	1800	2200
61-65	2000	2400	2600	61-65	1600	1800	2000
66-70	2000	2200	2600	66-70	1600	1800	2000
71-75	2000	2200	2600	71-75	1600	1800	2000
76 and up	2000	2200	2400	76 and up	1600	1800	2000

*Calorie levels are based on the Estimated Energy Requirements (EER) and activity levels from the Institute of Medicine Dietary Reference Intakes Macronutrients Report, 2002.
SEDENTARY = less than 30 minutes a day of moderate physical activity in addition to daily activities.
MOD. ACTIVE = at least 30 minutes up to 60 minutes a day of moderate physical activity in addition to daily activities.
ACTIVE = 60 or more minutes a day of moderate physical activity in addition to daily activities.

United StatesDepartment of Agriculture
Center for Nutrition Policy and Promotion
April 2005
CNPP-XX

Body Mass Index Table

Body Weight (pounds)

Category →	Normal						Overweight					Obese										Extreme Obesity														
BMI	19	20	21	22	23	24	25	26	27	28	29	30	31	32	33	34	35	36	37	38	39	40	41	42	43	44	45	46	47	48	49	50	51	52	53	54
Height (inches)																																				
58	91	96	100	105	110	115	119	124	129	134	138	143	148	153	158	162	167	172	177	181	186	191	196	201	205	210	215	220	224	229	234	239	244	248	253	258
59	94	99	104	109	114	119	124	128	133	138	143	148	153	158	163	168	173	178	183	188	193	198	203	208	212	217	222	227	232	237	242	247	252	257	262	267
60	97	102	107	112	118	123	128	133	138	143	148	153	158	163	168	174	179	184	189	194	199	204	209	215	220	225	230	235	240	245	250	255	261	266	271	276
61	100	106	111	116	122	127	132	137	143	148	153	158	164	169	174	180	185	190	195	201	206	211	217	222	227	232	238	243	248	254	259	264	269	275	280	285
62	104	109	115	120	126	131	136	142	147	153	158	164	169	175	180	186	191	196	202	207	213	218	224	229	235	240	246	251	256	262	267	273	278	284	289	295
63	107	113	118	124	130	135	141	146	152	158	163	169	175	180	186	191	197	203	208	214	220	225	231	237	242	248	254	259	265	270	278	282	287	293	299	304
64	110	116	122	128	134	140	145	151	157	163	169	174	180	186	192	197	204	209	215	221	227	232	238	244	250	256	262	267	273	279	285	291	296	302	308	314
65	114	120	126	132	138	144	150	156	162	168	174	180	186	192	198	204	210	216	222	228	234	240	246	252	258	264	270	276	282	288	294	300	306	312	318	324
66	118	124	130	136	142	148	155	161	167	173	179	186	192	198	204	210	216	223	229	235	241	247	253	260	266	272	278	284	291	297	303	309	315	322	328	334
67	121	127	134	140	146	153	159	166	172	178	185	191	198	204	211	217	223	230	236	242	249	255	261	268	274	280	287	293	299	306	312	319	325	331	338	344
68	125	131	138	144	151	158	164	171	177	184	190	197	203	210	216	223	230	236	243	249	256	262	269	276	282	289	295	302	308	315	322	328	335	341	348	354
69	128	135	142	149	155	162	169	176	182	189	196	203	209	216	223	230	236	243	250	257	263	270	277	284	291	297	304	311	318	324	331	338	345	351	358	365
70	132	139	146	153	160	167	174	181	188	195	202	209	216	222	229	236	243	250	257	264	271	278	285	292	299	306	313	320	327	334	341	348	355	362	369	376
71	136	143	150	157	165	172	179	186	193	200	208	215	222	229	236	243	250	257	265	272	279	286	293	301	308	315	322	329	338	343	351	358	365	372	379	386
72	140	147	154	162	169	177	184	191	199	206	213	221	228	235	242	250	258	265	272	279	287	294	302	309	316	324	331	338	346	353	361	368	375	383	390	397
73	144	151	159	166	174	182	189	197	204	212	219	227	235	242	250	257	265	272	280	288	295	302	310	318	325	333	340	348	355	363	371	378	386	393	401	408
74	148	155	163	171	179	186	194	202	210	218	225	233	241	249	256	264	272	280	287	295	303	311	319	326	334	342	350	358	365	373	381	389	396	404	412	420
75	152	160	168	176	184	192	200	208	216	224	232	240	248	256	264	272	279	287	295	303	311	319	327	335	343	351	359	367	375	383	391	399	407	415	423	431
76	156	164	172	180	189	197	205	213	221	230	238	246	254	263	271	279	287	295	304	312	320	328	336	344	353	361	369	377	385	394	402	410	418	426	435	443

Source: Adapted from Clinical Guidelines on the Identification, Evaluation, and Treatment of Overweight and Obesity in Adults: The Evidence Report.

Your Balanced Nutrition Plan: Two-Week Meal Plan

All of the meals meet the MyPyramid daily food group amounts based on 2,000 calories

Day 1

Breakfast

Orange juice, 1 cup   Instant oatmeal, 1 cup
Raisins, $\frac{1}{8}$ cup   Almonds, sliced, ½ ounce
Nonfat milk, 1 cup

Lunch

Healthy Choice Café Selections Chicken Basil Panini (1 Meal) or
    Chunky Butternut "Stew" with Couscous (see recipe on page 197)
4-ounce snack cup peaches, 1 each
Nonfat milk, 1 cup

Dinner

Healthy Choice Café Steamers Grilled Whiskey Steak (1 Meal) or Grilled
    Marinated Chicken with Tomato-Fruit Salsa (see recipe on page 199)
Whole-wheat dinner roll, 1 medium
Fleischmann's Original Stick Margarine, 1 teaspoon
Mixed salad greens, 1 cup, with:
    Cherry tomatoes, 5 each
    Sliced carrots, $\frac{1}{4}$ cup
    Sliced cucumber, unpeeled, $\frac{1}{4}$ cup
    Ranch salad dressing, 1 tablespoon
    Nonfat milk, 1 cup

Snack

Orville Redenbacher's Smart Pop popcorn, 1 serving
Apple, 1 each
Peter Pan Peanut Butter, creamy, 1 tablespoon

Nutrition Information per Day
Calories: 2,015; Calories from fat: 391 (19%); Fat: 43 g; Saturated Fat: 8 g; Cholesterol: 60 mg;
Sodium: 2,395 mg; Carbohydrates: 310 g; Dietary Fiber: 41 g; Calcium: 135 %DV; Iron: 54 %DV

MyPyramid Information
Fruits: 2 ¾ cups; Vegetables: $3^3/_4$ cups; Grains: $8^1/_2$ ounce equivalents; Meat & Beans: 5 ounce
equivalents; Milk: 3 ½ cups

Day 2

Breakfast

    Corn flakes, 1 cup

    Banana, 1 large

    David sunflower seeds, unsalted, $^1/_2$ ounce

    Nonfat milk, 1 cup

Lunch

    Tuna sandwich made with:

        Whole-grain bread, 2 slices

        Canned white tuna fish in water, drained, 2 ounces

        Light mayonnaise, 2 teaspoons

        Romaine lettuce, 1 leaf

        Tomato, 2 slices

        Provolone cheese, 1-ounce slice

    Blueberries, 1 cup

    Celery strips, 6 strips

    Raspberry yogurt parfait made with:

        Raspberry yogurt, low-fat, 1 each

        Granola, low-fat, ¼ cup

Dinner

    Healthy Choice Café Steamers General Tso's Spicy Chicken (1 meal) or Spicy

        Ginger Stir Fry (see recipe on page 203)

    Salad made with:

        Mixed salad greens, 2 cups

        Cherry tomatoes, $^1/_2$ cup

        Chopped red onion, 2 tablespoons

        Sliced water chestnuts, 1 ounce

        Asian sesame ginger salad dressing, 1 tablespoon

    Fortune cookie, 2 each

    Nonfat milk, 1 cup

Snack

        Mandarin oranges, canned, ½ cup

        David pumpkin seeds, kernels, unsalted, ½ ounce

        Gingersnap cookie, 1 each

Nutrition Information per Day

Calories: 1,935; Calories from fat: 330 (17%); Fat: 37 g; Saturated Fat: 6 g; Cholesterol: 60 mg; Sodium: 2,390 mg; Carbohydrates: 335 g; Dietary Fiber: 31 g; Calcium: 116 %DV; Iron: 133 %DV

MyPyramid Information

Fruits: 2 cups; Vegetables: $3^1/_2$ cups; Grains: 5 ounce equivalents; Meat & Beans: 6 ounce equivalents; Milk: $3^1/_2$ cups

Day 3

Breakfast

Cinnamon raisin bagel, toasted, 1 small
Peter Pan Peanut Butter, 1 tablespoon
Cubed fresh melon and cantaloupe, 1 cup
Nonfat milk, 1 cup

Lunch

Healthy Choice Café Selections Philly Cheese Steak Panini (1 meal) or Spicy Beef
    Noodle Salad (see recipe on page 202)
Grapes, 1 cup
Baby carrots, 1 cup
Nonfat milk, 1 cup

Dinner

Healthy Choice Complete Selections Four Cheese Manicotti (1 meal) or Angel Hair
    Pasta with Chicken and Shrimp (see recipe on page 204)
Salad made with:
    Chicken breast, grilled or roasted, skinless, 3 ounces
    Fresh spinach, 2 cups
    Sliced mushrooms, $^1/_2$ cup
    Sliced tomato, 1 each
Salad dressing made with:
    Olive oil, 1 tablespoon
    Balsamic vinegar, 2 teaspoons
    Dried herbs to taste

Garlic bread made with:
 Italian bread, 1 medium slice
 Fleischmann's Original Stick Margarine, 1 teaspoon
 Garlic powder, to taste
Nonfat milk, 1 cup

Snack
 Sliced banana, ½ cup
 Vanilla ice cream, ½ cup
 Chocolate syrup, 1 tablespoon
 Chopped walnuts, ½ ounce

Nutrition Information per Day
Calories: 1,996; Calories from fat: 488 (24%); Fat: 55 g; Saturated Fat: 15 g; Cholesterol: 147 mg; Sodium: 2,252 mg; Carbohydrates: 271 g; Dietary Fiber: 27 g; Calcium: 182 %DV; Iron: 65 %DV

MyPyramid Information
Fruits: 2½ cups; Vegetables: 4¼ cups; Grains: $7^1/_2$ ounce equivalents; Meat & Beans: 5½ ounce equivalents; Milk: 4 cups

Day 4

Breakfast

Yogurt vanilla nonfat, 1 cup, topped with:
> Granola, low-fat, ¼ cup
> Cranberry juice cocktail, 1 cup

Sliced strawberries, 1 cup
David sunflower seeds, unsalted, ½ ounce

Lunch

Healthy Choice Simple Selections Roast Turkey Breast (1 meal) or Corn Salad
> with Mesquite Turkey (see recipe on page 206)

Baby carrots, ½ cup
Sliced pepper, ½ cup
Nonfat milk, 1 cup

Dinner

Healthy Choice Complete Selections Fiesta Chicken (1 meal) or Fiesta Chicken
> (see recipe on page 207)

Salad made with:
> Chopped Romaine lettuce, 2 cups
> Sliced avocado, ½ cup
> Pinto beans, ¼ cup
> Ranch salad dressing, 1 tablespoon

Baked low-fat tortilla chips, 1 ounce
Nonfat milk, 1 cup

Snack

Peter Pan Peanut Butter, 1 tablespoon
Graham crackers, 2 each
Apple, 1 each

Nutrition Information per Day

Calories: 2,037; Calories from fat: 451 (22%); Fat: 50 g; Saturated Fat: 9 g; Cholesterol: 73 g;
Sodium: 2,223 mg; Carbohydrates: 323 g; Dietary Fiber: 37 g; Calcium: 135 %DV; Iron: 52 % DV

MyPyramid Information

Fruits: 3½ cups; Vegetables: 3 cups; Grains: 5 ounce equivalents; Meat & Beans: 5½ ounce
equivalents; Milk: 3 cups

Day 5

Breakfast

Whole-wheat English muffin, toasted, 1 each
Peter Pan Creamy Peanut Butter, 2 tablespoons
Orange, 1 large
Nonfat milk, 1 cup

Lunch

Curried Egg Salad (see recipe on page 198), 2 servings
Whole-grain bread, 2 slices
Cherry tomatoes, 1 cup
Nonfat milk, 1 cup

Dinner

Healthy Choice Complete Selections Classic Grilled Chicken BBQ (1 meal) or
    Buttermilk "Fried" Chicken (see recipe on page 196)
Cole slaw, $\frac{1}{4}$ cup
Yellow sweet corn on the cob, 1 each
Whole-wheat dinner roll, 1 small
Black cherry low-fat yogurt, 1 each

Snack

Sliced almonds, $\frac{1}{4}$ cup
Peach, 1 each
Brownie, small (2-inch) square

Nutrition Information per Day
Calories: 1,975; Calories from fat: 515 (26%); Fat: 57 g; Saturated Fat: 11 g; Cholesterol: 72 mg;
Sodium: 2,389 mg; Carbohydrates: 298 g; Dietary Fiber: 36 g; Calcium: 174 %DV; Iron: 86 %DV

MyPyramid Information
Fruits: $2\frac{1}{2}$ cups; Vegetables: $3\frac{3}{4}$ cups; Grains: 5 ounce equivalents; Meat & Beans: $8\frac{1}{2}$ ounce
equivalents; Milk: 3 cups

Day 6

Breakfast

Raspberry Protein Smoothie (see recipe on page 184), 1 serving
Whole-grain bread, toasted, 1 slice
Fleischmann's Margarine, 1 teaspoon

Lunch

Healthy Choice Café Steamers Grilled White Meat Chicken & Roasted Red Pepper
Alfredo (1 meal) or Baked Ziti Casserole (see recipe on page 194)
Diced cheddar cheese, $1\frac{1}{2}$ ounces
Grapes, 1 cup
Thin wheat crackers, 1 ounce

Dinner

Swordfish with Creole Relish (see recipe on page 184), 1 serving
Brown rice, 1 cup
Salad made with:
Mixed salad greens, 1 cup
Tomato, 1 each
Chopped sweet red bell pepper, $\frac{1}{2}$ cup
Low calorie French salad dressing, 2 tablespoons
Nonfat milk, 1 cup

Snack

Oatmeal raisin cookie, 2 each
Unsweetened applesauce, $\frac{1}{2}$ cup

Nutrition Information per Day
Calories: 2,054; Calories from fat: 468 (23%); Fat: 52 g; Saturated Fat: 19 g;
Cholesterol: 166 mg; Sodium: 2,360 mg; Carbohydrates: 302 g; Dietary Fiber: 22 g; Calcium: 117
%DV; Iron: 54 %DV

MyPyramid Information
Fruits: $2\frac{1}{4}$ cups; Vegetables: $2\frac{1}{2}$ cups; Grains: 5 ounce equivalents; Meat & Beans: $5\frac{1}{2}$ ounce
equivalents; Milk: 3 cups

Day 7

Breakfast

Breakfast Burritos with Tomato Basil (see recipe on page 185), 1 serving

Canned peach, ½ cup

Nonfat milk, 1 cup

Lunch

Healthy Choice Chicken & Dumpling Soup, 1 cup

Thin wheat crackers, 1 ounce

Apple slices, 1 cup

Celery strips, 1 cup

Peter Pan Peanut Butter, 2 tablespoons

Low-fat fruit yogurt, 1 each

Dinner

Turkey Marsala (see recipe on page 186), 1 serving

Spaghetti noodles, 1 cup

Steamed chopped broccoli, 1 cup

Nonfat milk, 1 cup

Snack

Orville Redenbacher's Smart Pop popcorn, 1 serving

Raisins, ¼ cup

Nutrition Information per Day

Calories: 1,934; Calories from fat: 271 (14%); Fat: 30 g; Saturated Fat: 8 g; Cholesterol: 87 mg; Sodium: 2,399 mg; Carbohydrates: 327 g; Dietary Fiber: 32 g; Calcium: 147 %DV; Iron: 71 %DV

MyPyramid Information

Fruits: 2 cups; Vegetables: 3 cups; Grains: 6 ounce equivalents; Meat & Beans: 6 ounce equivalents; Milk: 3 cups

Day 8

Breakfast

Bran flakes cereal, 1 cup

Banana, 1 large

Slivered almonds 1 ounce

Nonfat milk, 1 cup

Lunch

Tuna Salad made with:

Light tuna in water, drained, 2 ounces

Diced celery, $\frac{1}{4}$ cup

Chopped yellow onion, 1 tablespoon

Light mayonnaise, 1 tablespoon

Romaine lettuce, 1 leaf

Tomato, 2 slices

Provolone cheese, 1-ounce slice

Whole-grain bread, 2 slices

Low-sodium vegetable juice, 1 cup

Pineapple chunks in juice, drained, $\frac{1}{2}$ cup

Dinner

Black Beans and Mango Salad (see recipe on page 183), 1 serving

6-inch flour tortillas, 2 each

Avocado, sliced, 1 each

Nonfat chocolate milk, 1 cup

Snack

Sliced strawberries, $\frac{1}{2}$ cup

Chocolate syrup, 1 tablespoon

Reddi Wip Fat-Free Whipped Topping, 2 tablespoons

Chopped walnuts, ¼ ounce

Nutrition Information per Day

Calories: 1,984; Calories from fat: 724 (36%); Fat: 80 g; Saturated Fat: 15 g; Cholesterol: 49 mg; Sodium: 2,163 mg; Carbohydrates: 260 g; Dietary Fiber: 48 g; Calcium: 117 % DV; Iron: 128 % DV

MyPyramid Information

Fruits: $3\frac{1}{2}$ cups; Vegetables: $1\frac{1}{2}$ cups; Grains: 5 ounce equivalents; Meat & Beans: 5½ ounce equivalents; Milk: 3 cups

Day 9

Breakfast

Egg sandwich made with:

Whole-wheat English muffin, toasted, 1 each

Fleischmann's Original Margarine, 2 teaspoons

Egg Beaters Original cooked with PAM, $1/_2$ cup

Fresh oranges, 1 each

Nonfat milk, $1^1/_2$ cups

Lunch

Spinach Salad (see recipe on page 186), 1 serving

Healthy Choice Zesty Gumbo Soup, 1 cup

Thin wheat crackers, 1 ounce

Reduced-fat extra-sharp cheddar cheese, sliced, 1 ounce

Dinner

Baked Red Snapper (see recipe on page 187), 1 serving

Cooked brown rice, 1 cup

Low-sodium vegetable juice, 1 cup

Nonfat milk, 1 cup

Shortbread cookies, 2 each

Snack

Fruit cocktail, ½ cup

David sunflower seeds, unsalted kernels, ¼ ounce

Nutrition Information per Day

Calories: 1,935; Calories from fat: 552 (28%); Fat: 62 g; Saturated Fat: 15 g; Cholesterol: 80 mg; Sodium: 2,390 mg; Carbohydrates: 258 g; Dietary Fiber: 26 g; Calcium: 133 %DV; Iron: 76 %DV

MyPyramid Information

Fruits: 2 cups; Vegetables: 2½ cups; Grains: 5 ounce equivalents; Meat & Beans: 6 ounce equivalents; Milk: $3^1/_2$ cups

175

Day 10

Breakfast

Italian Omelet (see recipe on page 188), 1 serving
Whole-grain bread toasted, 1 slice
Fleischmann's Margarine, 1 teaspoon
100% apple juice, 1$^1/_2$ cups

Lunch

Healthy Choice Café Selections Smoked Chicken Panini (1 meal) or
    Broccoli-Cheddar Egg Puff (see recipe on page 195)
Baby carrots, 1 cup
Celery strips, 3 pieces
Canned peaches, ½ cup
Nonfat vanilla yogurt, ½ cup

Dinner

Savory Pizza Meatloaf (see recipe on page 189), 1 serving
Baked potato, 1 large
Fleischmann's Original Stick Margarine, 2 teaspoons
Cooked green beans, 1 cup
Whole-wheat dinner roll, 1 medium
Nonfat chocolate milk, 1 cup

Snack

Unsalted roasted peanuts, ¼ ounce
Raisins, ¼ cup
Wheat Squares cereal, ½ cup

Nutrition Information per Day
Calories: 1,975; Calories from fat: 310 (16%); Fat: 35 g; Saturated Fat: 10 g; Cholesterol: 91 mg; Sodium: 2,350 mg; Carbohydrates: 318 g; Dietary Fiber: 32 g; Calcium: 138 %DV; Iron: 123 %DV

MyPyramid Information
Fruits: 2$^1/_2$ cups; Vegetables: 3$^1/_4$ cups; Grains: 6 ounce equivalents; Meat & Beans: 6 ounce equivalents; Milk: 2 cups

Day 11

Breakfast

Plain instant oatmeal, 1 cup, topped with:

Maple syrup, 1 tablespoon

Fleischmann's Original Stick Margarine, 1 teaspoon

Chopped walnuts, ½ ounce-weight

Orange juice, 1 cup

Nonfat milk, 1½ cups

Lunch

Healthy Choice Simple Selections Salisbury Steak (1 meal) or Jamaican Beef and
Broccoli (see recipe on page 200)

Whole-wheat dinner roll, 1 each

Pineapple chunks, drained, 1 cup

Nonfat chocolate milk, 1 cup

Dinner

Three-Cheese Stuffed Manicotti (see recipe on page 190), 1 serving

Garlic bread made with:

Italian bread, 1 piece

Fleischmann's Margarine, 1 tablespoon

Garlic powder to taste

Salad made with:

Fresh spinach, 2 cups

Chopped hard boiled eggs, 1 each

David sunflower seeds kernels, unsalted, ½-ounce weight

Oil and vinegar salad dressing, 2 tablespoons

Snack

Peter Pan Peanut Butter, 1 tablespoon

Apple slices, 1 cup

Graham cracker, 1 each

Nutrition Information per Day

Calories: 2,602; Calories from fat: 702 (27%); Fat: 78 g; Saturated Fat: 16 g; Cholesterol: 233 mg;
Sodium: 2,146 mg; Carbohydrates: 250 g; Dietary Fiber: 25 g; Calcium: 124 %DV; Iron: 80 %DV

MyPyramid Information

Fruits: 3 cups; Vegetables: 2 ¾ cups; Grains: 6 ounce equivalents; Meat & Beans: 6 ounce
equivalents; Milk: 3 cups

Day 12

Breakfast

Whole-grain cereal, 1 cup

Slivered Almonds, ½ ounce

Cubed fresh melon and cantaloupe, 1 cup

Nonfat milk, 1½ cups

Lunch

Healthy Choice Café Steamers Beef Merlot (1 meal) or

Southwestern Fajita Quiche (see recipe on page 201)

Whole-wheat dinner roll, 1 small

Apple, 1 large

Nonfat milk, 1½ cups

Dinner

Fresh Vegetable Crisp (see recipe on page 191), 3 servings

Caesar Salad made with:

Chopped Romaine lettuce, 2 cups

Skinless grilled or roasted chicken, 3 ounces

Caesar salad dressing, 2 tablespoons

Cherry tomatoes, ½ cup

Snack

Hummus, 2 tablespoons

Whole-wheat pita bread, 1 each

Apple juice, 1 cup

Nutrition Information per Day

Calories: 1,993; Calories from fat: 458 (23%); Fat: 51 g; Saturated Fat: 10 g; Cholesterol: 118 mg; Sodium: 2,533 mg; Carbohydrates: 285 g; Dietary Fiber: 31 g; Calcium: 122 %DV; Iron: 76 %DV

MyPyramid Information

Fruits: 3 cups; Vegetables: 3½ cups; Grains: 4½ ounce equivalents; Meat & Beans: 7 ounce equivalents; Milk: 3 cups

Day 13

Breakfast

Nonfat vanilla yogurt, 1 each
Low-fat granola, $\frac{1}{2}$ cup
Sliced strawberries, 1 cup

Lunch

Healthy Choice Café Steamers Grilled Chicken Marinara (1 meal) or Chicken
Florentine (see recipe on page 205)
Fresh tomato and mozzarella salad made with:
Mozzarella cheese, freshwater-packed, 2 ounces
Sliced tomato, 1 each
Olive oil, 1 tablespoon
Chopped fresh basil, 1 teaspoon
Black pepper, $\frac{1}{8}$ teaspoon
Italian bread, 2 medium slices
Apple juice, 1 cup

Dinner

Hebrew National 97% Fat-Free Kosher Beef Franks, 1 each
Whole-grain hot dog bun, 1 each
Chopped tomato, $\frac{1}{2}$ medium
Chopped yellow onion, 1 teaspoon
Pickle relish, 1 teaspoon
Van Camp's Baked Beans Original, ¼ cup
Chocolate nonfat milk, 1 cup

Snack

Canned pears, 1 cup, topped with:
Chocolate syrup, 1 tablespoon
Chopped walnuts, ½-ounce weight

Nutrition Information per Day
Calories: 1,941; Calories from fat: 419 (22%); Fat: 47 g; Saturated Fat: 13 g;
Cholesterol: 68 mg; Sodium: 2,297 mg; Carbohydrates: 311 g; Dietary Fiber: 24 g;
Calcium: 122 %DV; Iron: 68 %DV

MyPyramid Information
Fruits: 3 cups; Vegetables: 2$\frac{1}{2}$ cups; Grains: 5$\frac{1}{2}$ ounce equivalents; Meat & Beans: 4½ ounce
equivalents; Milk: 3 cups

Day 14

Breakfast

Toasted whole-grain bread, 2 slices
Peter Pan Peanut Butter, 2 tablespoons
Orange, 1 each
Nonfat milk, 1 cup

Lunch

Healthy Choice Complete Selections Lemon Pepper Fish (1 meal) or Blackened
Salmon with Warmed Fruit Salsa (see recipe on page 192)
Orville Redenbacher's Smart Pop Butter popcorn* 94% Fat-Free,
1 serving, with raisins , $^1/_2$ cup
Nonfat milk, $1^1/_2$ cups

Dinner

Asian Grilled Flank Steak (see recipe on page 193), 1 serving
Cooked brown rice, $^1/_2$ cup
Baby carrots, 1 cup
Sliced red bell pepper, ½ cup
Ranch salad dressing, 2 tablespoons

Snack

Snack Pack Vanilla pudding, 1 each
Banana slices, ¼ cup
Reddi Wip Fat-Free Whipped topping, 2 tablespoons

Nutrition Information per Day
Calories: 2,045; Calories from fat: 490 (24%); Fat: 55 g; Saturated Fat: 12 g; Cholesterol: 96 mg;
Sodium: 2,482 mg; Carbohydrates: 314 g; Dietary Fiber: 31 g; Calcium: 113 %DV; Iron: 75 %DV

MyPyramid Information
Fruits: $2^1/_4$ cups; Vegetables: 2 cups; Grains: $6^1/_2$ ounce equivalents; Meat & Beans: 7 ounce
equivalents; Milk: $2^1/_2$ cups

Balanced Meal Planner

Day	Breakfast	Lunch	Dinner	Snack
Day 1				
Day 2				
Day 3				
Day 4				
Day 5				
Day 6				
Day 7				

Shopping List:

_____

_____

_____

_____

_____

_____

_____

_____

_____

_____

_____

_____

_____

Recipes

Black Beans and Mango Salad

Number of servings: 6

$1/_4$	cup chopped fresh peppermint	2	(15-ounce) cans Ranch Style Black Beans, rinsed and drained
2	tablespoons low-sodium chicken broth		
2	tablespoons lime juice	$1/_3$	cup chopped green onions
1	tablespoon extra-virgin olive oil	6	leaves Bibb lettuce
1	teaspoon ground coriander	2	medium kiwis, peeled and sliced
1	teaspoon granulated sugar	1	mango, peeled and sliced
$1/_8$	teaspoon ground nutmeg		

1. In a medium bowl, combine the mint, broth, lime juice, oil, coriander, sugar, and nutmeg, and beat with a wire whisk until well blended. Add the beans; toss to coat. Cover. Let stand 1 hour, stirring occasionally.
2. Add the onions; mix lightly.
3. Cover 6 serving plates with the lettuce; top with the bean mixture. Arrange the kiwi and mango slices around the bean mixture. Garnish with additional mint, if desired.

Nutrition Information per Serving:
Calories: 177; Calories from fat: 29 (16%); Fat: 3g; Saturated Fat: 0g; Cholesterol: 0mg; Sodium: 466mg; Carbohydrates: 32g; Dietary Fiber: 7g; Calcium: 3%DV; Iron: 11%DV

MyPyramid Information
Fruits: ½ cups; Vegetables: 0 cups; Grains: 0 ounce equivalents; Meat & Beans: 1 ounce equivalents; Milk: 0 cups

Raspberry Protein Smoothie

Number of servings: 1

8 ounces low-fat red raspberry yogurt
$1/_2$ cup raspberries in light syrup, thawed
$1/_4$ cup Egg Beaters 100% Egg Whites

$1/_4$ cup chilled orange juice
1 ounce fat-free Reddi-Wip

1. Place the yogurt, raspberries, Egg Beaters, and orange juice in a blender container. Cover and blend on medium speed until smooth.
2. Pour into a tall glass and top with Reddi-Wip.

Nutrition Information per Serving
Calories: 432; Calories from fat: 41 (9%); Fat: 5g; Saturated Fat: 2g; Cholesterol: 20mg; Sodium: 246mg; Carbohydrates: 82g; Dietary Fiber: 0g; Calcium: 27%DV; Iron: 6%DV

MyPyramid Information
Fruits: $3/_4$ cup; Vegetables: 0 cups; Grains: 0 ounce equivalents; Meat & Beans: 1 ounce equivalent; Milk: 1 cup

Swordfish with Creole Relish

Number of servings: 4

$1/_2$ cup chopped tomatoes
$1/_4$ cup chopped red bell peppers
1 teaspoon Pure Wesson Vegetable Oil
$1/_4$ cup diced celery
$1/_4$ cup chopped yellow onion
4 teaspoons fresh lemon juice, divided
1 teaspoon minced garlic
$1/_2$ teaspoon dried oregano

$1/_4$ teaspoon ground basil
$1/_4$ teaspoon ground thyme
$1/_4$ teaspoon granulated sugar
$1/_8$ teaspoon salt
1 teaspoon hot pepper sauce (optional)
4 (4-ounce) swordfish steaks
PAM Original Cooking Spray
2 lemon wedges, peeled (optional)

1. Preheat the broiler. Place the tomatoes and bell peppers in a blender container; cover. Blend until almost smooth; set aside.
2. Add the oil to a small nonstick skillet; heat over medium heat 1 minute. Add the celery, onion, 1 teaspoon of the lemon juice, and the garlic; cook 7 minutes, or until the vegetables are crisp-tender, stirring frequently. Add the tomato mixture, oregano, basil, thyme, sugar, and salt; mix well. Season with the hot pepper sauce, if desired. Cook 4 minutes, or until thickened, stirring frequently. Remove from the heat; cover to keep warm.

3. Cut each fish steak crosswise in half. Spray a broiler pan and rack with cooking spray. Place the fish on the rack; sprinkle evenly with the remaining 3 teaspoons lemon juice.

4. Broil, 4 to 6 inches from the heat, 4 to 6 minutes, or until the fish flakes easily with a fork. Top each fish steak with about 2 tablespoons of the tomato mixture. Serve with lemon wedges, if desired.

Nutrition Information per Serving
Calories: 169; Calories from fat: 55 (33%); Fat 6g; Saturated Fat: 1g; Cholesterol: 44mg; Sodium: 214mg; Carbohydrates: 4g; Dietary Fiber: 1g; Calcium: 2%DV; Iron: 6%DV

MyPyramid Information
Fruits: 0 cups; Vegetables: ¼ cups; Grains: 0 ounce equivalents; Meat & Beans: 2½ ounce equivalents; Milk: 0 cups

Breakfast Burritos with Tomato Basil

Number of servings: 4

PAM Original Cooking Spray
1   cup Southern-style hash brown potatoes
¼   cup chopped white onion
1   cup Egg Beaters Original
⅛   teaspoon black pepper

1   tomato, chopped
2   teaspoons chopped fresh basil
4   flour tortillas
½   cup shredded mild cheddar cheese

1. Spray a medium nonstick skillet with cooking spray; heat over medium heat. Add the hash browns and onion; cook 9 minutes, or until the potatoes are golden brown, stirring frequently.

2. Add the Egg Beaters and pepper; mix well. Cook 3 minutes, or until the Egg Beaters are slightly set; stir. Cook an additional 6 minutes, or until the Egg Beaters reach the desired doneness, stirring occasionally.

3. Combine the tomato and basil; set aside. Spoon the Egg Beaters mixture evenly down the center of the tortillas; top with the cheese and tomato mixture. Fold in the opposite sides of each tortilla; roll up burrito-style.

Nutrition Information per Serving
Calories: 245; Calories from fat: 60 (24%); Fat: 7g; Saturated Fat: 3g; Cholesterol: 10mg; Sodium: 399mg; Carbohydrates: 33g; Dietary Fiber: 2g; Calcium: 14%DV; Iron: 17%DV

MyPyramid Information
Fruits: 0 cups; Vegetables: ½ cup; Grains: 1 ounce equivalent; Meat & Beans: 1 ounce equivalents; Milk: ¼ cup

Turkey Marsala

Number of servings: 5

$\frac{1}{3}$ cup sweet Marsala dessert wine	1 tablespoon chopped fresh parsley
$\frac{1}{4}$ cup low-sodium chicken broth	$\frac{1}{4}$ teaspoon black pepper
1 tablespoon cornstarch	PAM Original Cooking Spray
8 ounces fresh sliced mushrooms	$19\frac{1}{2}$ ounces boneless turkey breast
$\frac{1}{2}$ medium carrot, sliced	tenderloins

1. Mix the wine, broth, and cornstarch in a small bowl until well blended; set aside.
2. Spray a large nonstick skillet with cooking spray; heat over medium heat. Add the mushrooms, carrot, parsley, and the broth mixture; stir. Cook 6 minutes, or until the mushrooms are tender and the sauce is thickened and translucent, stirring constantly.
3. Sprinkle the pepper evenly over the turkey breasts. Add to the skillet; turn to evenly coat both sides of the tenderloins with the sauce. Cover; reduce the heat to low. Cook 25 minutes, or until the tenderloins are no longer pink in the center and the juices run clear (170°F), turning occasionally. Garnish with additional chopped fresh parsley, if desired.

Nutrition Information per Serving
Calories: 165; Calories from fat: 17 (10%); Fat: 2g; Saturated Fat: 0g; Cholesterol: 44mg; Sodium: 75mg; Carbohydrates: 6g; Dietary Fiber: 1g; Calcium: 0%DV; Iron: 11%DV

MyPyramid Information
Fruits: 0 cups; Vegetables: ½ cup; Grains: 0 ounce equivalents; Meat & Beans: 4 ounce equivalents; Milk: 0 cups

Spinach Salad

Number of servings: 4

2 tablespoons golden seedless raisins	1 cup chopped dried pears
2 tablespoons chopped shallots	1 cup chopped apples
2 tablespoons fresh lemon juice	$\frac{1}{4}$ cup olive oil
2 tablespoons red wine vinegar	$\frac{1}{8}$ teaspoon black pepper
6 cups chopped spinach	2 ounces chopped walnuts

1. Make the dressing by combining in a small bowl the raisins, shallots, lemon juice, and red wine vinegar, and let stand 10 minutes.
2. In a large bowl, combine the spinach, pears, and apples.
3. Whisk the olive oil into the dressing. Pour the dressing over the salad and toss.
4. Season with the pepper, and top with the walnuts.

Nutrition Information per Serving
Calories: 385; Calories from fat: 207 (54%); Fat: 23g; Saturated Fat: 3g; Cholesterol: 0mg; Sodium: 41mg; Carbohydrates: 46g; Dietary Fiber: 6g; Calcium: 6%DV; Iron: 17%DV

MyPyramid Information
Fruits: ½ cup; Vegetables: ¾ cup; Grains: 0 ounce equivalents; Meat & Beans: 1 ounce equivalent; Milk: 0 cups

Baked Red Snapper

Number of servings: 4

PAM Original Cooking Spray		$^1/_4$	cup chopped fresh parsley
1	pound snapper fillets	$^1/_2$	teaspoon paprika
$^1/_2$	cup chopped shallots	$^1/_2$	teaspoon ground cumin seeds
1	clove garlic, chopped	$^1/_8$	teaspoon black pepper
1	teaspoon extra-virgin olive oil	2	tomatoes, chopped
$^1/_4$	cup fresh lemon juice	2	cups chopped spinach

1. Preheat the oven to 350°F. Spray an 8x8-inch baking dish with cooking spray. Place the fish, skin side down, in the prepared dish. Set aside.
2. Combine the shallots, garlic, and oil in a medium nonstick skillet. Cook over medium heat 3 to 4 minutes, or until the shallots are crisp-tender, stirring frequently. Remove from the heat. Stir in the lemon juice, parsley, paprika, cumin seeds, and pepper. Pour the sauce over the fish; top with the tomatoes. Cover.
3. Bake 5 minutes, or until the fish flakes easily when tested with a fork. Serve over the spinach, and garnish with additional parsley, if desired.

Nutrition Information per Serving
Calories: 164; Calories from fat: 28 (17%); Fat: 3g; Saturated Fat: 1g; Cholesterol: 42mg; Sodium: 94mg; Carbohydrates: 9g; Dietary Fiber: 2g; Calcium: 6%DV; Iron: 6%DV

MyPyramid Information
Fruits: 0 cups; Vegetables: ¾ cup; Grains: 0 ounce equivalents; Meat & Beans: 2 ½ ounce equivalents; Milk: 0 cups

Italian Omelet

Number of servings: 2

2 teaspoons sliced black olives
$1/_2$ teaspoon chopped canned pimiento
$1/_2$ cup reduced-fat ricotta cheese
1 teaspoon chopped fresh basil
$1/_4$ teaspoon garlic powder
$1/_8$ teaspoon black pepper

PAM Original Cooking Spray
1 cup Egg Beaters Original
2 tablespoons shredded Parmesan
cheese
$1/_4$ cup canned pasta sauce

1. Blot the olives and pimiento with a paper towel to remove excess moisture. In a small mixing bowl, combine the olives, pimiento, ricotta cheese, basil, garlic powder, and pepper. Set aside.
2. Spray a 10-inch nonstick skillet with cooking spray. Heat the skillet over medium heat. Pour the Egg Beaters into the skillet. Lift the edge of the cooked Egg Beaters with a spatula and tilt the skillet to allow uncooked egg product to run to the bottom of the skillet. Cook $1^1/_2$ to $2^1/_2$ minutes, or until the omelet is still moist, but nearly set.
3. Spread the cheese mixture evenly over the bottom half of the omelet. Loosen the side of the omelet with a spatula. Fold the top half over the bottom half. Cook 2 to 3 minutes, or until the filling is hot and the omelet is set. Slide the omelet onto a serving plate.
4. In a 1-quart saucepan, heat the pasta sauce over medium heat 1 to 2 minutes, or until hot, stirring occasionally. Spoon the sauce over the omelet. Garnish with the shredded Parmesan cheese.

Nutrition Information per Serving
Calories: 160; Calories from fat: 39 (24%); Fat: 4g; Saturated Fat: 2g; Cholesterol: 19mg; Sodium: 492mg; Carbohydrates: 9g; Dietary Fiber: 1g; Calcium: 16%DV; Iron: 17%DV

MyPyramid Information
Fruits: 0 cups; Vegetables: 0 cups; Grains 0 ounce equivalents; Meat & Beans: 2 ounce equivalents; Milk: 1 cup

Savory Pizza Meatloaf

Number of servings: 6

PAM Original Cooking Spray

1 pound 95% lean ground beef

$\frac{1}{2}$ cup bread crumbs

$\frac{1}{3}$ cup Egg Beaters Original

$\frac{2}{3}$ cup Hunt's Family Favorite Pizza Sauce, divided

$\frac{1}{4}$ cup fat-free shredded mozzarella cheese

1. Preheat the oven to 350°F. Spray a 9x5-inch loaf pan with cooking spray; set aside. In a bowl, mix the ground beef, bread crumbs, Egg Beaters, and $\frac{1}{3}$ cup of the pizza sauce.
2. Shape into an oblong loaf; place into the prepared dish.
3. Bake 50 minutes. Pour the remaining $\frac{1}{3}$ cup pizza sauce over the meatloaf; sprinkle with the cheese. Bake an additional 10 minutes, or until the center is no longer pink. Let stand 10 minutes before cutting into six slices to serve.

Nutrition Information per Serving
Calories: 195; Calories from fat: 48 (25%); Fat: 5g; Saturated Fat: 2g; Cholesterol: 56mg; Sodium: 399mg; Carbohydrates: 10g; Dietary Fiber: 1g; Calcium: 5%DV; Iron: 22%DV

MyPyramid Information
Fruits: 0 cups; Vegetables: 0 cups; Grains: 0 ounce equivalents; Meat & Beans: 3 ounce equivalents; Milk: 0 cups

Three-Cheese Stuffed Manicotti

Number of servings: 4

8 manicotti shells

$1^3/_4$ cups canned pasta sauce, divided

1 (10-ounce) package frozen chopped spinach, thawed, drained, and squeezed dry

1 cup fat-free ricotta cheese

$^1/_4$ cup Egg Beaters 100% Egg Whites

1 tablespoon shredded Parmesan cheese

$^1/_4$ teaspoon garlic powder

$^1/_2$ cup low-moisture, part-skim shredded mozzarella cheese

1. Heat oven to 400°F. Prepare the manicotti shells as directed on the package. Drain and rinse. Let stand in warm water.
2. Spread $^3/_4$ cup of the pasta sauce in a 12x8-inch baking dish. Set aside.
3. Combine the spinach, ricotta cheese, Egg Beaters, Parmesan cheese, and garlic powder in a medium mixing bowl. Drain the manicotti shells. Stuff each shell with a heaping $^1/_4$ cup spinach mixture. Arrange the stuffed shells over the sauce in the prepared baking dish.
4. Spoon the remaining 1 cup pasta sauce over the shells. Cover with foil. Bake 15 to 20 minutes, or until the sauce bubbles. Sprinkle with the mozzarella cheese. Bake, uncovered, 5 to 7 minutes, or until the cheese is melted.

Nutrition Information per Serving
Calories: 292; Calories from fat: 40 (14%); Fat: 4g; Saturated Fat: 2g; Cholesterol: 19mg; Sodium: 581mg; Carbohydrates: 43g; Dietary Fiber: 5g; Calcium: 28%DV; Iron: 17%DV

MyPyramid Information
Fruits: 0 cups; Vegetables: 1 cup; Grains: 1 ounce equivalent; Meat & Beans: 0 ounce equivalents; Milk: ¾ cup

Fresh Vegetable Crisp

Number of servings: 6

2 (7- to 8-inch) flour tortillas	$1/_8$ teaspoon garlic powder
PAM Original Cooking Spray	4 cups water
3 ounces fat-free cream cheese	1 cup broccoli florets
6 tablespoons low-fat shredded cheddar cheese, divided	$1/_2$ cup sliced mushrooms
$1/_2$ teaspoon dried basil	$1/_2$ cup sliced red bell peppers

1. Preheat a medium nonstick skillet over medium heat. Lightly spray both sides of one tortilla with cooking spray. Place in the skillet; cook 3 minutes on each side, or until lightly browned on both sides. Remove from the skillet. Repeat with the remaining tortilla.
2. Preheat oven to 350°F. In a small bowl, combine the cream cheese, 2 tablespoons of the cheddar cheese, basil, and garlic powder. Spread the mixture evenly over one of the tortillas; top with the remaining tortilla. Place on a baking sheet; set aside.
3. Pour the water into a medium saucepan. Bring to a boil over high heat. Add the broccoli; cook 1 minute or until the color brightens. Remove with a slotted spoon; plunge immediately into ice water. Drain.
4. Top the tortilla with the broccoli, mushrooms and bell peppers; sprinkle with the remaining 4 tablespoons cheddar cheese.
5. Bake 8 minutes, or until the cheese is melted and the vegetables are crisp-tender. Cut into six wedges to serve.

Nutrition Information per Serving
Calories: 88; Calories from fat: 16 (18%); Fat: 2g; Saturated Fat: 1g; Cholesterol: 4mg; Sodium: 198mg; Carbohydrates: 12g; Dietary Fiber: 1g; Calcium: 7%DV; Iron: 6%DV

MyPyramid Information
Fruits: 0 cups; Vegetables: ¾ cup; Grains: 1½ ounce equivalents; Meat & Beans: 0 ounce equivalents; Milk: ½ cup

Blackened Salmon with Warmed Fruit Salsa

Number of servings: 8 (1 salmon fillet with $\frac{1}{4}$ cup salsa each)

1 medium mango, peeled and chopped	2 tablespoons ground white pepper
1 small papaya, peeled, seeded, and chopped	2 tablespoons garlic powder
	2 tablespoons onion powder
2 tablespoons minced red onion	1 tablespoon ground mustard
1 tablespoon orange juice	2 $\frac{1}{2}$ teaspoons ground red pepper
1 tablespoon fresh lime juice	2 $\frac{1}{2}$ teaspoons ground thyme
1 (14.5-ounce) can Hunt's Petite Diced Tomatoes, drained	8 salmon fillets, skin removed and patted dry
$\frac{1}{4}$ cup paprika	PAM Professional No-Stick Cooking Spray
2 tablespoons ground black pepper	1 tablespoon chopped fresh cilantro
2 tablespoons kosher salt	1 $\frac{1}{2}$ teaspoons chopped fresh mint

1. Preheat the oven to 425°F. Combine the mango, papaya, onion, orange juice, lime juice, and tomatoes in a medium bowl. Gently toss to coat and set aside.
2. Blend the paprika, black pepper, salt, white pepper, garlic powder, onion powder, ground mustard, red pepper, and thyme in a small bowl. Place $\frac{1}{4}$ cup of the spice blend onto a plate. Store the remaining spice blend in an airtight container for future use.
3. Press one side of each salmon fillet lightly into the spice blend. Remove and shake off any excess seasoning; set aside. Discard the remaining seasoning used to coat the salmon.
4. Spray a large ovenproof skillet with cooking spray. Turn on the stove vent. Heat the skillet over high heat. When the skillet is hot, add the salmon fillets, in batches, seasoned side down. Cook 1 to 2 minutes or until the seasoning has darkened and formed a crust. Turn; cook 1 to 2 minutes longer or until golden brown. Transfer the seared fillets to a sheet pan. Place the pan into the preheated oven; bake 3 to 5 minutes or until the salmon has reached an internal temperature of 145°F.
5. Place the fruit salsa in a separate skillet; cook, stirring occasionally over medium heat 3 to 5 minutes or until the tomatoes are warmed through. Sprinkle with the chopped cilantro and mint. Serve immediately with salmon.

Nutrition Information per Serving:
Calories: 100; Calories from fat: 45 (45%); Total Fat: 5g; Saturated Fat: 0.5g; Cholesterol: 60mg; Sodium: 270mg; Total Carbohydrate 13g; Dietary Fiber: 2g; Protein 23g; Calcium: 4%DV; Iron: 8%DV

MyPyramid Information
Fruits: $^1/_4$ cup; Vegetables: ¼ cup; Grains: 0 ounce equivalents; Meat & Beans: 1 ounce equivalent; Milk: 0 cups

Asian Grilled Flank Steak

Number of servings: 4

2	tablespoons rice vinegar	$^1/_4$	teaspoon chopped fresh rosemary
1 $^1/_2$	tablespoons light soy sauce	$^1/_8$	teaspoon crushed red chili pepper flakes
1	tablespoon balsamic vinegar	$^1/_8$	teaspoon black pepper
$^1/_2$	teaspoon ginger root	16	ounces flank steak
$^1/_4$	teaspoon sesame oil	1	cup quick-cooking brown rice
1	clove of garlic, chopped	$^1/_4$	cup chopped green onions

1. In a bowl, combine the rice vinegar, soy sauce, balsamic vinegar, ginger root, sesame oil, garlic, rosemary, red chili pepper, and black pepper. Add the steak to the marinade and marinate in the refrigerator for at least 1 hour or overnight, turning occasionally.
2. In a small saucepan, cook the rice according to the directions on the package, omitting any salt or fat.
3. Preheat the grill. Grill the flank steak 4 to 8 minutes on each side, depending on the desired degree of doneness.
4. Let the steak rest on a carving plate for 1 to 2 minutes. Slice the steak on the bias.
5. Toss the rice with the green onions and serve with the steak.

Nutrition Information per Serving
Calories: 315; Calories from fat: 59 (19%); Fat: 7g; Saturated Fat: 2g; Cholesterol: 60mg; Sodium: 480mg; Carbohydrates: 24g; Dietary Fiber: 2g; Calcium: 4%DV; Iron: 17%DV

MyPyramid Information
Fruits: 0 cups; Vegetables: 0 cups; Grains: ¾ ounce equivalent; Meat & Beans: 3 ounce equivalents; Milk: 0 cups

Baked Ziti Casserole

Number of servings: 6 (1 1/4 cups each)

PAM Original Cooking Spray
8 ounces ziti pasta
1 pound lean ground beef
1 (26-ounce) can Hunt's Four Cheese
   Spaghetti Sauce

1 (6-ounce) can Hunt's Tomato Paste
1 cup shredded mozzarella cheese

1. Preheat the oven to 350°F. Spray an 8x8-inch baking dish with cooking spray. Prepare the pasta according to the package directions; drain.
2. Cook the beef in a large skillet over medium-high heat 7 minutes, or until browned and crumbled, stirring frequently; drain. Stir in the spaghetti sauce and tomato paste; blend well.
3. Spoon $\frac{1}{2}$ cup meat sauce into the bottom of the prepared baking dish. Layer with half the pasta, half the meat sauce, and $\frac{1}{2}$ cup cheese. Repeat the layers, ending with the cheese.
4. Bake, uncovered, 10 minutes or until the cheese is melted. Serve immediately.

Nutrition Information per Serving:
Calories: 390; Calories from fat: 108 (28%); Total Fat: 12g; Saturated Fat: 5g; Cholesterol: 59mg; Sodium: 791mg; Total Carbohydrate 43g; Dietary Fiber: 6g; Protein 29g; Calcium: 15%DV; Iron: 34%DV

MyPyramid Information
Fruits: 0 cups; Vegetables: ¾ cup; Grains: 1½ ounce equivalents; Meat & Beans: 1½ ounce equivalents; Milk: ¼ cup

Broccoli-Cheddar Egg Puff

Number of servings: 8

PAM Original Cooking Spray
1 $1/_2$ teaspoons Pure Wesson Canola Oil
2 cups chopped broccoli florets
$1/_2$ cup chopped onion
$1/_2$ cup chopped red bell pepper

1 $3/_4$ cups skim milk
1 $1/_2$ cups Egg Beaters Original
1 cup reduced-fat baking mix
$3/_4$ cup (3 ounces) shredded cheddar cheese

1. Preheat oven to 350°F. Spray an 8x8-inch baking dish with cooking spray.
2. Heat the oil in a medium nonstick skillet over medium-high heat. Add the broccoli, onion, and red pepper; cook and stir 4 minutes, or until crisp-tender. Remove from the heat.
3. Combine the milk, Egg Beaters, baking mix, and about half the cheese in a large bowl. Beat with a wire whisk until blended. Add the vegetables; mix lightly. Pour the mixture into the prepared baking dish.
4. Bake 40 minutes. Sprinkle the top with the remaining cheese. Bake another 10 minutes, or until a knife inserted in the center comes out clean. Cool 5 minutes.

Nutrition Information per Serving:
Calories: 170; Calories from fat: 50 (29%); Total Fat: 5g; Saturated Fat: 2.5g; Cholesterol: 10mg; Sodium: 350mg; Total Carbohydrate 18g; Dietary Fiber: 2g; Protein 12g; Calcium: 20%DV; Iron: 10%DV

MyPyramid Information
Fruits: 0 cups; Vegetables: ½ cup; Grains: ½ ounce equivalent; Meat & Beans: 1 ounce equivalents; Milk: ½ cup

Buttermilk "Fried" Chicken

Number of servings: 6

6	boneless, skinless chicken breasts (about 2 pounds)	$^1/_2$	teaspoon salt
$^3/_4$	cup low-fat buttermilk	$^1/_2$	teaspoon ground black pepper
$^1/_2$	cup Egg Beaters 100% Egg Whites	$^1/_2$	teaspoon ground red pepper
1	cup all-purpose flour	$^1/_2$	teaspoon paprika
$^1/_3$	cup cornmeal	3	tablespoons Pure Wesson Canola Oil
			PAM Original Cooking Spray

1. Preheat the oven to 400°F. Pound the chicken with a meat mallet to even thickness.
2. Whisk the buttermilk and Egg Beaters together in shallow dish. In a separate shallow dish, combine the flour, cornmeal, salt, black pepper, red pepper, and paprika; mix well.
3. Dip the chicken in the buttermilk mixture then dredge in the flour mixture. Cook the chicken in two batches. For each batch, heat $1^1/_2$ tablespoons oil in a large nonstick skillet over medium-high heat. Add three of the chicken breasts to the skillet. Cook 4 minutes on each side or until browned. Repeat with the remaining three chicken breasts. Transfer the chicken to a baking sheet sprayed with cooking spray; bake 8 to 10 minutes or until done.

Nutrition Information per Serving:
Calories: 280; Calories from fat: 80 (29%); Total Fat: 9g; Saturated Fat: 1g; Cholesterol: 90mg; Sodium: 200mg; Total Carbohydrate 10g; Dietary Fiber: 1g; Protein 37g; Calcium: 4%DV; Iron: 10%DV

MyPyramid Information
Fruits: 0 cups; Vegetables: 0 cups; Grains: ½ ounce equivalent; Meat & Beans: 3½ ounce equivalents; Milk: 0 cups

Chunky Butternut "Stew" with Couscous

Number of servings: 7

1	butternut squash (about 2 pounds), halved lengthwise and seeded
2	tablespoons Wesson Pure Canola Oil
1	large onion, chopped
3	cloves of garlic, minced
$1/_2$	teaspoon cayenne pepper
$1/_8$	teaspoon ground cinnamon
$1/_8$	teaspoon ground nutmeg
1	teaspoon cumin, divided
2	(14-ounce) cans reduced-sodium chicken broth
1	(15-ounce) can garbanzo beans, rinsed and drained
1	(14.5-ounce) can Hunt's Petite Diced Tomatoes, drained
$1/_2$	cup raisins
$1/_2$	teaspoon kosher salt, divided
$1^1/_2$	cups water
$1^1/_2$	cups (9 ounces) dry couscous
2	tablespoons chopped fresh parsley
$1/_4$	cup chopped almonds

1. Peel the squash. Cut into 1-inch chunks; set aside.
2. Heat the oil in a 6-quart saucepan over medium heat. Add the onion; cook and stir occasionally until soft, about 5 minutes. Stir in the garlic, cayenne pepper, cinnamon, nutmeg, and $1/_2$ teaspoon of the cumin. Cook for 1 minute.
3. Add the broth, squash, beans, drained tomatoes, raisins, and $1/_4$ teaspoon of the salt. Bring to a boil. Reduce the heat to low. Cover and cook 10 minutes. Remove the lid and cook until the squash is tender, about 15 minutes.
4. Bring the water to boil in a medium saucepan. Stir in the remaining $1/_2$ teaspoon cumin and the remaining $1/_4$ teaspoon salt. Add the couscous. Cover and remove from the heat. Let stand about 5 minutes. Fluff with a fork.
5. In a shallow serving bowl, ladle the stew over the couscous. Sprinkle the top with the parsley and almonds.

Nutrition Information per Serving:
Calories: 370; Calories from fat: 60 (16%); Total Fat: 7g; Saturated Fat: 1g; Cholesterol: 0mg; Sodium: 580mg; Total Carbohydrate 68g; Dietary Fiber: 8g; Protein 11g; Calcium: 15%DV; Iron: 15%DV

MyPyramid Information
Fruits: ¼ cup; Vegetables: ¾ cup; Grains: 1½ ounce equivalents; Meat & Beans: 1 ounce equivalent; Milk: 0 cups

Curried Egg Salad

Number of servings: 4

PAM Original Cooking Spray
1 cup Egg Beaters Original
2 tablespoons reduced-fat mayonnaise
2 tablespoons plain nonfat yogurt
$^1/_4$ teaspoon curry powder
1 cup halved red seedless grapes

$^1/_4$ cup chopped celery
2 green onions, sliced
4 leaves Boston lettuce
2 tablespoons slivered almonds, toasted

1. Spray a two-cup glass measuring cup with cooking spray. Add the Egg Beaters; cover. Microwave on high 1 minute; stir with a fork. Microwave an additional 45 seconds, or until the center is set.
2. Place the cooked Egg Beaters in a medium bowl. Using a fork, break the egg into bite-size pieces. Let stand 15 minutes, or until cool.
3. Add the mayonnaise, yogurt, curry powder, grapes, celery, and onions; mix lightly. Serve over the lettuce leaves. Sprinkle evenly with the almonds.

Nutrition Information per Serving:
Calories: 100; Calories from fat: 25 (25%); Total Fat: 3g; Saturated Fat: 0g; Cholesterol: 0mg; Sodium: 190mg; Total Carbohydrate 11g; Dietary Fiber: 1g; Protein 8g; Calcium: 6%DV; Iron: 8%DVV

MyPyramid Information
Fruits: ½ cup; Vegetables: ½ cup; Grains: 0 ounce equivalents; Meat & Beans: 2½ ounce equivalents; Milk: 0 cups

Grilled Marinated Chicken with Tomato-Fruit Salsa

Number of servings: 6

2   cloves of garlic, finely chopped
$\frac{1}{4}$ cup Hunt's ketchup
$\frac{1}{4}$ cup Worcestershire sauce
$\frac{1}{4}$ cup white wine vinegar
$\frac{1}{4}$ cup honey
2   tablespoons LaChoy Lite Soy Sauce
6   boneless, skinless chicken breasts
     ($1\frac{1}{2}$ pounds)

PAM for Grilling spray
1   (14.5-ounce) can Hunt's Petite Diced
     Tomatoes, drained
1   cup diced pineapple, mango, or papaya
$\frac{1}{4}$ cup chopped red onion
1   tablespoon chopped fresh cilantro

1. Combine the garlic, ketchup, Worcestershire sauce, vinegar, honey, and soy sauce in a small bowl; mix well. Pound the chicken with a meat mallet to even thickness. Place the chicken in a large resealable bag. Pour the marinade into the bag, turning the chicken pieces to evenly coat. Seal the bag. Refrigerate at least 2 hours or overnight.
2. Spray a cold grill and utensils with grilling spray. Preheat the grill to medium heat. Combine the diced tomatoes, pineapple, onion, and cilantro in a small bowl; set aside. Remove the chicken from the bag; discard the marinade.
3. Grill the chicken 5 minutes; turn. Cook an additional 5 minutes, or until no longer pink in the center. Serve each chicken breast with $\frac{1}{3}$ cup of the tomato-fruit salsa.

Nutrition Information per Serving:
Calories: 180; Calories from fat: 15 (8%); Total Fat: 1.5g; Saturated Fat: 0g; Cholesterol: 65mg; Sodium: 460mg; Total Carbohydrate 15g; Dietary Fiber: 1g; Protein 27g; Calcium: 4%DV; Iron: 8%DV

MyPyramid Information
Fruits: ¼ cup; Vegetables: 1¼ cups; Grains: 0 ounce equivalents; Meat & Beans: 2½ ounce equivalents; Milk: 0 cups

Jamaican Beef and Broccoli

Number of servings: 4

2 cups (8 ounces) broccoli florets	1 (11-ounce) can Mandarin oranges,
PAM Original Cooking Spray	drained
1 pound top sirloin steak, cut into thin strips	3 tablespoons Caribbean Jerk Marinade
$1/_4$ teaspoon ground black pepper	3 cups hot cooked brown rice
$1/_2$ onion, chopped (about 1 cup)	
1 (14.5-ounce) can Hunt's Diced Tomatoes, drained	

1. Place the broccoli and 1 tablespoon of water in a microwavable bowl; cover with a lid. Microwave on high 1 minute; drain and set aside.
2. Spray a large nonstick skillet with cooking spray. Heat over medium-high heat for 1 minute. Cook the steak in the skillet 5 minutes or until browned, stirring frequently; remove from the pan. Add the pepper and onion; cook 5 minutes or until browned, stirring often. Return the steak to the skillet. Add the drained tomatoes, broccoli, Mandarin oranges, and marinade. Simmer over low heat 10 minutes, or until the sauce is hot and thickened, stirring occasionally.
3. Serve over the brown rice.

Nutrition Information per serving:
Calories: 340; Calories from fat: 45 (13%); Total Fat: 5g; Saturated Fat: 1.5g; Cholesterol: 40mg; Sodium: 580mg; Total Carbohydrate 44g; Dietary Fiber: 5g; Protein 31g; Calcium: 10%DV; Iron: 15%DV

MyPyramid Information
Fruits: ¼ cup; Vegetables: ¼ cup; Grains: 1 ounce equivalent; Meat & Beans: 2½ ounce equivalents; Milk: 0 cups

Southwestern Fajita Quiche

Number of servings: 8 (1 slice each)

PAM Original Cooking Spray
$^1/_2$ cup thinly sliced red bell pepper
$^1/_2$ cup thinly sliced green bell pepper
$^1/_3$ cup thinly sliced onion
4 ounces boneless, skinless chicken breasts, cut into strips
1 cup Egg Beaters Southwestern

$^3/_4$ cup skim milk
$^1/_2$ teaspoon ground cumin
1 cup reduced-fat shredded Mexican cheese blend
4 (8-inch) flour tortillas
Salsa (optional)
Fat-free sour cream (optional)

1. Preheat the oven to 350°F. Spray a medium skillet with cooking spray. Heat over medium heat.
2. Add the bell peppers and onion; cook 5 minutes or until crisp-tender. Remove from the pan and set aside. Stir in the chicken and cook 3 minutes, or until the chicken is no longer pink. Remove from the pan and set aside with the peppers and onion.
3. Combine the Egg Beaters, milk, and cumin in a large bowl. Add the cheese; mix lightly. Stir in the cooked peppers, onion, and chicken.
4. Spray a 9-inch pie plate with cooking spray. Place the tortillas in the pie plate to form a crust, evenly overlapping each other (allowing 3 to 4 inches to overlap the top of pie plate). Carefully pour the Egg Beater mixture into the tortilla crust. Bake 40 minutes, or until a knife inserted in the center comes out clean. Cool on a wire rack 10 minutes before serving. Serve with salsa and fat-free sour cream, if desired.

Nutrition Information per Serving:
Calories: 160; Calories from fat: 45 (28%); Total Fat: 5g; Saturated Fat: 2g; Cholesterol: 20mg; Sodium: 370mg; Total Carbohydrate 15g; Dietary Fiber: 1g; Protein 13g; Calcium: 20%DV; Iron: 8%DV

MyPyramid Information
Fruits: 0 cups; Vegetables: 0 cups; Grains: ½ ounce equivalent; Meat & Beans: 1 ounce equivalent; Milk: ½ cup

Spicy Beef Noodle Salad

Number of servings: 4 (1 cup each)

4	ounces uncooked rice noodles	2	green onions, sliced diagonally
2	tablespoons peanut oil	$1/_2$	cup grated carrots
1	tablespoon hot chili sauce	$1/_2$	cup julienned red bell pepper
1	tablespoon honey	$1/_2$	cup julienned English cucumber
1	tablespoon fresh lime juice	8	ounces flank steak, thinly sliced across
1	tablespoon seasoned rice vinegar		the grain
2	teaspoons La Choy Lite Soy Sauce	$1/_2$	teaspoon kosher salt
1	teaspoon toasted sesame oil	$1/_4$	teaspoon ground black pepper
1	teaspoon fish sauce		PAM Professional Cooking Spray
1	tablespoon chopped fresh cilantro	2	tablespoons La Choy Crispy Rice
$1/_2$	teaspoon grated fresh ginger root		Noodles

1. Prepare the rice noodles according to the package directions, omitting the salt. Drain; set aside.
2. Whisk the peanut oil, chili sauce, honey, lime juice, rice vinegar, soy sauce, sesame oil, fish sauce, cilantro, and ginger in a large bowl. Add the green onions, carrots, bell pepper, cucumber, and prepared rice noodles to the mixture; set aside.
3. Season the steak with salt and black pepper. Spray a 12-inch skillet with cooking spray. Heat over high heat. When hot, add the steak. Cook and stir about 4 minutes or until the steak is still pink in the center. Cook in batches, if needed, to prevent overcrowding.
4. Add the beef to the bowl. Toss to coat all the ingredients evenly with the dressing.
5. Garnish with the crispy noodles. Serve at room temperature. Refrigerate leftovers.

Nutrition Information per Serving:
Calories: 300; Calories from fat: 100 (33%); Total Fat: 12g; Saturated Fat: 3g; Cholesterol: 15mg; Sodium: 520mg; Total Carbohydrate 33g; Dietary Fiber: 2g; Protein 15g; Calcium: 4%DV; Iron: 10%DV

MyPyramid Information
Fruits: 0 cups; Vegetables: ½ cup; Grains: 1 ounce equivalent; Meat & Beans: 1½ ounce equivalents; Milk: 0 cups

Spicy Ginger Stir Fry

Number of servings: 6 (1 cup each)

$^1/_3$ cup La Choy Garlic Ginger Stir-Fry Sauce

$^1/_3$ cup reduced-sodium chicken broth

$^1/_4$ cup orange juice

1 teaspoon crushed red pepper flakes

1 teaspoon cornstarch

PAM Professional Cooking Spray

12 ounces boneless, skinless chicken breasts, cut into bite-size pieces

1 tablespoon grated ginger root

2 teaspoons minced garlic

12 ounces broccoli florets, cut into bite-size pieces

8.8 ounces (1 package) whole-grain brown rice, prepared

3 tablespoons finely chopped crystallized ginger

2 tablespoons finely chopped toasted walnuts

$^1/_2$ teaspoon toasted sesame oil

1. Whisk the stir-fry sauce, broth, juice, pepper flakes, and cornstarch together in a small bowl until smooth; set aside.

2. Spray a wok or 12-inch skillet with cooking spray; place over high heat. When hot, add the chicken. Cook and stir 3 to 5 minutes, or until the chicken is light golden brown. Add the ginger root and garlic; cook and stir 1 minute, or until aromatic.

3. Add the broccoli florets; cook and stir 3 to 5 minutes, or until the broccoli turns bright green and is crisp-tender. Blend in the sauce mixture and cook 2 to 3 minutes or until the sauce has thickened slightly.

4. Add the rice, crystallized ginger, walnuts, and sesame oil. Toss to blend all of the ingredients. Heat through and serve immediately.

Nutrition Information per Serving:
Calories: 270; Calories from fat: 40 (15%); Total Fat: 4.5g; Saturated Fat: 0.5g; Cholesterol: 35mg; Sodium: 380mg; Total Carbohydrate 41g; Dietary Fiber: 3g; Protein 17g; Calcium: 6%DV; Iron: 10%DV

MyPyramid Information
Fruits: 0 cups; Vegetables: ¾ cup; Grains: ½ ounce equivalent; Meat & Beans: 1½ ounce equivalents; Milk: 0 cups

Angel Hair Pasta with Chicken and Shrimp

Number of servings: 4 (1$\frac{1}{2}$ cups each)

6 ounces angel hair pasta	1 medium yellow crookneck squash, cut
$\frac{1}{2}$ cup chicken broth	into $\frac{1}{4}$-inch-thick slices
2 tablespoons La Choy Lite Soy Sauce	1 small red or green bell pepper, cut into
2 teaspoons cornstarch	thin strips
$\frac{1}{2}$ teaspoon ground ginger	8 ounces boneless, skinless chicken
PAM Olive Oil Cooking Spray	breasts, cut into $\frac{3}{4}$-inch pieces
$\frac{1}{2}$ cup sliced green onions	4 ounces peeled and deveined shrimp
2 cloves of garlic, minced	

1. Cook the pasta according to the package directions, omitting any salt or fat; drain.
2. Meanwhile, in a small bowl, combine the broth, soy sauce, cornstarch, and ginger using a wire whisk until well blended; set aside. Spray a large skillet with cooking spray. Heat 1 minute over medium-high heat. Add the onions and garlic; cook 1 to 2 minutes, or until the garlic is golden brown, stirring occasionally. Remove the onions and garlic from the skillet; set aside.
3. Add the squash to the skillet; cook 2 minutes, stirring frequently. Add the bell pepper; cook 2 minutes, or until the vegetables are crisp-tender, stirring frequently. Remove the vegetables from the skillet; set aside. Add the chicken and shrimp to the skillet; cook 3 to 4 minutes, or until the chicken is no longer pink in the center and the shrimp turn pink. Push the chicken and shrimp to one side of the skillet. Stir the broth mixture; pour into the skillet. Cook 1 minute, or until the broth mixture is thickened, stirring constantly. Mix in the cooked vegetables; cook 1 to 2 minutes, or until heated through, stirring frequently.
4. Drain the pasta; place on a serving plate. Spray with cooking spray; top with the chicken, shrimp, and vegetable mixture.

Nutrition Information per Serving:
Calories: 278; Calories from fat: 27 (10%); Total Fat: 3g; Saturated Fat: 1g; Cholesterol: 66mg; Sodium: 476mg; Total Carbohydrate 39g; Dietary Fiber: 3g; Protein 23g; Calcium: 4%DV; Iron: 16%DV

MyPyramid Information
Fruits: 0 cups; Vegetables: ½ cup; Grains: 1½ ounce equivalents; Meat & Beans: 2 ounce equivalents; Milk: 0 cups

Chicken Florentine

Number of servings: 6 (1 chicken breast half each)

PAM Original Cooking Spray
1   cup shredded Parmesan cheese
$^1/_2$ teaspoon Italian seasoning
6   (6-ounce) boneless, skinless chicken breasts
1   tablespoon Parkay Original Spread

$^1/_4$ cup sliced green onions
$^1/_2$ cup skim milk
$^2/_3$ cup chopped spinach, squeezed dry
1   (2-ounce) jar chopped pimientos, drained
$^1/_8$ teaspoon salt

1. Preheat the oven to 350°F. Spray a 13x9-inch baking dish with cooking spray.
2. Combine the cheese and Italian seasoning in a shallow dish. Add the chicken; turn to evenly coat both sides. Arrange the chicken in the prepared baking dish. Set aside the remaining cheese mixture for later use.
3. Melt the Parkay in a small saucepan over medium heat. Add the onions and cook 2 minutes, or until tender, stirring occasionally. Add the milk and cook until thickened, stirring frequently. Add the spinach, pimientos, and salt; mix well. Spoon the sauce over the chicken; top with the remaining cheese mixture.
4. Bake 30 to 35 minutes, or until the chicken is no longer pink in the center and the juices run clear (165°F).

Nutrition Information per Serving:
Calories: 345; Calories from fat: 99 (29%); Total Fat: 11g; Saturated Fat: 4g; Cholesterol: 144mg; Sodium: 439mg; Total Carbohydrate 3g; Dietary Fiber: 1g; Protein 56g; Calcium: 26%DV; Iron: 13%DV

MyPyramid Information
Fruits: 0 cups; Vegetables: ¼ cup; Grains: 0 ounce equivalents; Meat & Beans: 3½ ounce equivalents; Milk: ½ cup

205

Corn Salad with Mesquite Turkey

Number of servings: 4 (1 cup corn, $\frac{1}{2}$ cup spinach, and $1\frac{1}{2}$ ounces turkey each)

$\frac{1}{3}$	cup light Italian dressing	$\frac{1}{2}$	cup chopped red bell pepper
$\frac{1}{2}$	teaspoon ground cumin	2	tablespoons chopped fresh cilantro
3	cups frozen whole kernel corn, thawed	2	cups torn fresh spinach leaves
1	cup chopped celery	6	ounces thinly sliced mesquite turkey

1. Mix the dressing and cumin in a small bowl; set aside. Combine the corn, celery, bell pepper, and cilantro in a large bowl. Add the dressing mixture; toss to coat.
2. Cover four salad plates with the spinach leaves. Cut the turkey into strips; arrange evenly over the spinach.
3. Top each salad with about 1 cup of the corn mixture just before serving.

Nutrition Information per Serving:
Calories: 191; Calories from fat: 45 (24%); Total Fat: 5g; Saturated Fat: 1g; Cholesterol: 21mg; Sodium: 550 mg; Total Carbohydrate 29g; Dietary Fiber: 4g; Protein 11g; Calcium: 4%DV; Iron: 7%DV

MyPyramid Information
Fruits: 0 cups; Vegetables: 1¾ cups; Grains: 0 ounce equivalents; Meat & Beans: 1½ ounce equivalents; Milk: 0 cups

Fiesta Chicken

Number of servings: 8 (1 drumstick and $^3/_4$ cup rice each)

1 $^1/_2$ teaspoons Pure Wesson Vegetable Oil

2 $^1/_2$ pounds chicken drumsticks (about 8)

3 $^1/_2$ tablespoons thinly sliced green onions

2 (10-ounce) cans Ro-Tel Original Diced Tomatoes & Green Chilies, undrained

1 cup uncooked long grain white rice

1 (8-ounce) can Hunt's Tomato Sauce

$^1/_2$ cup water

$^1/_2$ cup (2 ounces) shredded cheddar cheese

1. Heat the oil in a large skillet over medium-high heat. Add the chicken; cook until golden brown on all sides, turning occasionally. Remove the chicken from the skillet, reserving the drippings in the skillet; cover the chicken to keep warm.
2. Reserve 2 tablespoons of the green onions for later use. Add the remaining onions to the drippings in the skillet; mix well. Stir in the tomatoes and juice, the rice, tomato sauce, and water. Bring to a boil. Top with the chicken; cover. Reduce the heat to low; simmer 20 minutes, or until the drumsticks are no longer pink in the center and the juices run clear (165°F).
3. Top the chicken with the cheese and the reserved 2 tablespoons green onions; cover. Cook an additional 5 minutes, or until the cheese is melted, the liquid is absorbed, and the rice is tender.

Nutrition Information per Serving:
Calories: 302; Calories from fat: 99 (33%); Total Fat: 11g; Saturated Fat: 4g; Cholesterol: 73mg; Sodium: 550mg; Total Carbohydrate 24g; Dietary Fiber: 1g; Protein 24g; Calcium: 8%DV; Iron: 13%DV

MyPyramid Information
Fruits: 0 cups; Vegetables: ½ cup; Grains: 1 ounce equivalent; Meat & Beans: 3 ounce equivalents; Milk: 0 cups

Nutrition Tips

Fruit Fiesta

- Sweeten sliced fresh strawberries with a small amount of preserves or fruit syrups mixed with a splash of balsamic vinegar for a healthy dessert. The combination of tastes really heightens the berry flavor while adding less sugar.
- Do you love fresh berries with ice cream? Spare the fat and calories by choosing a low-fat ice cream or frozen yogurt. Or, for a special treat, top the berries with a few tablespoons of melted regular vanilla ice cream. You'll enjoy much of the same flavor with a lower fat intake.
- Enhance the flavor, fiber, and nutrients of your morning bowl of cereal by adding fresh or frozen blueberries, strawberries, raspberries, peaches, or bananas.
- If you have bananas that are going to turn brown before they are used, slice and freeze to use in smoothies or baked goods.

Veggie Variety Show

- Spinach is great in salad and can add interest and nutrients to other foods. Use it on sandwiches, add it to pasta dishes, or stir it into soups.
- To add fiber, taste, texture, and great appearance, add drained and rinsed black beans to tacos, fajitas, and salsas.
- Add shredded or chopped carrots to prepared spaghetti sauce for extra sweetness and nutrition. Sautéed green and red peppers or zucchini also zip up the sauce.
- Think color when choosing vegetables and fruit. Brightly colored vegetables and fruits are typically rich in many nutrients, including vitamins, antioxidants, and other phytochemicals.
- Grilling and vegetables go together. Make a veggie kabob of onion chunks, green and red pepper squares, mushrooms, and cherry

tomatoes. Slice medium yellow squash and zucchini length-wise, and slice eggplant in circles. Brush the sliced vegetables and kabobs with the olive oil, and grill until tender. Best position on the grill is off direct heat.

- For a cold summer soup, experiment with gazpacho. All you need is fresh tomato chunks, peeled cucumber chunks, green pepper, and a little olive oil and garlic. Throw them in the food processor or blender and process until smooth. Add low-sodium vegetable juice if needed for consistency or thicken with a slice or two of bread. Season with fresh ground pepper, sea salt, and low-fat plain yogurt.
- Use puréed cooked carrots, tomatoes, broccoli, cauliflower, or turnips to thicken a soup or as a sauce to add nutrients. Select taste and color to blend with the soup or dish you're preparing.

Time Savers

- To reduce time during busy weekdays for meal prep, take time on the weekend to get ahead of tasks:
    - Cut/slice/chop all your vegetables and store them in resealable plastic bags to save space, or buy precut/prewashed vegetables.
    - Cook pasta needed for the entire week in a large batch; drain and cool it; then spray with a little non-stick spray and toss to keep from sticking. Store in resealable plastic bags until needed.
    - For a fast alternative to rice or pasta, try couscous. Like pasta, couscous is made from semolina wheat and is available in a precooked, dry form that takes only minutes to prepare with boiling water. For added flavor with little added sodium or calories, use low-sodium broth, peach tea, or even fruit juice as the cooking liquid. Add nutrition, color and texture by including shredded carrots, sliced green onion, chopped dried apricots, raisins, or dried cranberries.

Whole-Grain Goodness

- Pop some popcorn—it's a whole grain that can be easily incorporated into a balanced eating plan. Choose low-fat microwave varieties.
- Instant oatmeal is a speedy way to have whole grains in the morning. Serve with fat-free milk and fruit to get three nutritious food groups.
- Look for whole-grain versions of favorites such as pasta, waffles, or rice dishes.
- Add barley to your favorite vegetable soups for a whole-grain boost.
- Summer salad treats: Try tabbouli with bulgar wheat, tomatoes, cukes, garlic, and parsley and drizzled with lemon juice and olive oil. Or try quinoa or barley instead of bulgar.
- In a favorite waffle, pancake, or quick bread recipe, substitute whole-wheat flour for up to half the amount of flour required.

Lean Protein

- Fish is a great "fast" food that's good for you. The rule of thumb for cooking fish: Cook it ten minutes for every inch of thickness. So a half-inch thick piece of fish should take five minutes to cook; a one-inch-thick piece will take about ten minutes to cook.
- Poaching is great way to cook chicken breasts or fish without adding fat. The food is gently simmered in a liquid. Cooking liquids may include stock, wine, lemon or other fruit juices, or water. Combine different liquids and add in herbs or other seasonings for a greater variety of flavor options.
- Control portions for both adults and kids by making individual, mini meatloaves. Use your favorite meatloaf recipe (use ground turkey instead of beef) and bake it in a muffin pan instead of a loaf pan.

Kid Pleasers

- For a quick, nutritious after-school snack or dessert, top pudding or gelatin with fresh fruit.
- Keep cocoa mix with added calcium on hand. For a richer flavor and an extra calcium boost, make it with nonfat milk instead of water.
- For colorful after-school snacks, serve red, yellow, or green bell pepper strips in addition to carrot and celery sticks, with a small amount of dressing for dipping.
- For a kids' sleepover or Saturday afternoon with friends, have a "make your own pizza party." Use pita bread or English muffin halves as crust, with prepared spaghetti sauce, low-fat shredded mozzarella cheese and a variety of other toppings (mushrooms, ham and pineapple, etc.). Bake in a toaster oven until cheese is melted.
- Add peanut butter to celery stalks for a fun snack with fiber and protein. Top with raisins for "ants on a log" or fish-shaped cheese crackers for "swimming fish."
- To make Goofy Grins, cut a red-skinned apple into wedges, and then spread peanut butter on one side of each wedge. Place two or three mini marshmallows between the "buttered" wedges for teeth.

Lazy Breakfasts

- Involve kids in meal preparation by having them make Breakfast Banana Splits. Use bananas, a variety of flavored yogurts, and toppings such as cereal, canned pineapple, raisins, and sunflower seeds. Top with fruit syrup.
- For a healthier breakfast alternative, make French toast using multigrain bread and egg white–based egg substitute.
- Make a great-tasting fruit syrup for pancakes or waffles; use it instead of butter. Mash a ripe banana in a small saucepan, add orange juice to cover, and heat until bubbling. If you made the syrup

too thin, cook a minute or two to reduce; too thick, add more juice. Try it over pancakes made with low-fat milk. Or spoon it over frozen whole-grain waffles.

Keep Fat Balanced

- When a recipe calls for cream and you're watching your calorie and fat intake, use nonfat half-and-half or evaporated skim milk.
- If you are going to cook with fat, choose an oil high in monounsaturated fat such as canola oil or olive oil in place of butter.
- To minimize calories while keeping food from sticking to skillets and woks, use a cooking spray instead of oil. It also helps reduce clean up time.
- You can reduce fat while boosting flavor by combining mayonnaise with an equal amount of seasoned rice vinegar. Use the blend in mayonnaise-based salads or on its own as a sandwich spread. It adds flavor while only contributing half the fat of regular mayonnaise.
- To add crunch to taco salad without a lot of fat and salt, cut strips of corn tortilla, spray them with cooking spray, and stir-fry in a nonstick skillet until crisp. Top salad as desired; store leftovers in an airtight container.

Salad Strategies

Because they offer the crunch and color of nutritious, low-fat vegetables, many people turn to salads when they're trying to eat healthier. Unfortunately, yummy add-ons and dressing can turn a nutritious salad into a high-fat indulgence. Here are simple suggestions for making a delicious, satisfying salad that is loaded with great nutrition:

- For great nutrition, texture, and visual appeal, substitute dark green leaf lettuce for iceberg lettuce as the foundation for your salad.
- Add a variety of vegetables for dining satisfaction. Try chopped yellow or red bell pepper, jicama, slices of red onion, mushrooms, corn, grilled/roasted vegetables, sweet grape tomatoes, cucumbers, sliced strawberries/mangoes/oranges/crisp apples, dried fruit.
- A sensible salad makes a nutritious meal with the addition of protein. Some possible additions include grilled lean steak, chicken, shrimp or tofu; seasoned lean ground beef or turkey; rinsed and drained black beans/kidney beans/garbanzo beans. Add leftover cooked rice or cooked and cubed redskin or sweet potatoes. Serve them hot on the cool, crisp greens!
- You can add flavorful fun to a salad while still keeping the fat and calories in check. Choose only one of the following and only use a small amount: crisp, crumbled bacon; a sprinkle of full-flavored aged cheese such as blue cheese, Parmesan, or shredded sharp cheddar cheese; toasted nuts; soy nuts; sunflower kernels; chopped hard-cooked egg; sliced avocado; or ripe olives.
- You can make or break the nutritional goodness of your salad by adding a healthy dressing or drowning it in a dressing with too much fat. Here are several ideas for controlling the amount of fat being added to your salad without sacrificing taste:
  - Toss the salad completely after adding dressing. If the dressing is well distributed, you won't need as much. Use a shallow, wide salad bowl and drizzle a small, pre-measured amount of dressing over the entire surface. Then toss the salad thoroughly to ensure that the dressing is well distributed. Add additional dressing in small increments and toss until optimal amount has been added.
  - Make your own vinaigrette using a good quality virgin olive oil and experimenting with different types of vinegar to see what you prefer. Consider aged balsamic vinegar, wine vinegar, or the lighter seasoned rice vinegar. Typically, vinaigrette uses three

parts oil to one part vinegar. When you use milder vinegar, you may be happy with equal parts oil to vinegar—or even less.

- Use a favorite full-fat prepared salad dressing but blend it with equal parts wine vinegar or rice vinegar before adding to your salad. This will cut fat in half yet provide plenty of dressing to combine with salad.
- Cut the fat but not the flavor of prepared ranch dressing by combining a small bottle of dressing with a ten-ounce can of diced tomatoes and green chilies, drained. The tomatoes add a delicious spiciness. This is especially good for taco salads … and for dipping, too!
- Enjoy salad for lunch at work. Pack salad fixings in a one- to two-gallon resealable plastic bag. Just before serving, add salad dressing and shake to combine. Pour dressed salad into serving bowl—no extra utensils to clean or dirty hands!

Recommended Resources

Web Sites

Government General Health and Medical Information

    http://medlineplus.gov—National Library of Medicine

    http://health.nih.gov—National Institutes of Health

    www.healthfinder.gov—National Health Information Service

    www.cdc.gov—Centers for Disease Control and Prevention

    www.fitness.gov—President's Council on Physical Fitness and
        Sports

    www.MyPyramid.gov—U.S. Department of Agriculture
        and Health and Human Services

    www.nutrition.gov—U.S. Department of Agriculture

Heath-Care Associations or Agencies

    http://familydoctor.org—American Academy of Family Physicians

    www.ama-assn.org—American Medical Association

    www.americanheart.org—American Heart Association

    www.apahelpcenter.org—American Psychological Association
        Help Center

    www.lungusa.org—American Lung Association

    www.cancer.org—American Cancer Society

    www.eatright.org—American Dietetic Association

Commercial Sites

    www.webmd.com—WebMD

    www.mayoclinic.com—The Mayo Clinic

    www.rippehealth.com—Ripe Health Institute

    www.supplementwatch.com—Supplement Watch

Books

Anderson, Bob. *Stretching*. California: Shelter Publications, 2000.

Duyff, Roberta Larsen. *American Dietetic Association Complete Food and Nutrition Guide, Third Edition*. New York: Wiley, 2006.

Kabat-Zinn, Jon. *Full Catastrophe Living: Using the Wisdom of Your Body and Mind to Face Stress, Pain, and Illness*. New York: Delta, 1990.

Kabat-Zinn, Jon. *Wherever You Go, You Are There: Mindfulness Meditation in Everyday Life*. New York: Hyperion, 1995.

Moore, Thomas. *Care of the Soul: A Guide for Cultivating Depth and Sacredness in Everyday Life*. New York: HarperCollins, 1992.

Peck, M. Scott. *The Road Less Traveled: A New Psychology of Love, Traditional Values and Spiritual Growth, 25th anniversary edition*. New York: Touchstone, 1993.

Rippe, James M., M.D. *High Performance Health: 10 Real Life Solutions to Redefine Your Health and Revolutionize Your Life*. Nashville: Thomas Nelson, 2007

Siegel, Bernie S. *Love, Medicine and Miracles:Lessons Learned about Self-Healing from a Surgeon's Experience with Exceptional Patients*. New York: Harper, 1990.

Siegel, Bernie S. *Peace, Love and Healing: Bodymind Communication & the Path to Self-Healing: An Exploration*. New York: Harper, 1990.

Notes

Chapter 1

1. KT Knoops et al., "Mediterranean diet, lifestyle factors, and 10-year mortality in elderly European men and women: the HALE project," *JAMA* 292, no. 12 (2004):1433–9.

2. TM Manini et al., "Daily activity energy expenditure and mortality among older adults," *JAMA* 296, no. 2 (2006):171–9.

3. NT Lautenschlager and OP Almeida, "Physical activity and cognition in old age," *Current Opinions in Psychiatry* 19, no. 2 (2006):190–3.

Chapter 2

1. Centers for Disease Control, National Center for Health Statistics, "FastFacts A-Z, Death/Mortality 2004 data," http://www.cdc.gov/nchs/fastats/lcod.htm (accessed August 2, 2007).

2. Healthy People 2010. "Chapter 22, Physical Activity and Fitness," http://www.healthypeople.gov/Document/HTML/Volume2/22Physical.htm#_Toc490380795 (accessed August 2, 2007).

3. Centers for Disease Control, "Fruit and Vegetable Consumption Among Adults— United States 2005," *Morbidity and Mortality Weekly Report*, March 30, 2007, 56 no. 10, Centers for Disease Control, http://www.cdc.gov/mmwr/preview/mmwrhtml/mm5610a2.htm (accessed August 2, 2007).

4. Weight Information Network of NIDDK of National Institutes of Health, "Prevalence Statistics Related to Overweight and Obesity," National Institutes of Health, http://win.niddk.nih.gov/statistics/index.htm#preval (accessed August 2, 2007).

5. American Psychological Association, "Facts and Statistics: Stress," American Psychological Association, http://www.apahelpcenter.org/articles/topic.php?id=6#Stress (accessed August 2, 2007).

Chapter 3

1. Adapted from Center for Disease Control, Division of Nutrition, Physical Activity and Obesity. Access at: http://www.cdc.gov/nccdphp/dnpa/physical/starting/index.htm.

Chapter 6

1 SM Krebs-Smith, P Kris-Etherton, "How does MyPyramid compare to other population-based recommendations for controlling chronic disease?" *Journal of the American Dietetic Association* 107, no. 5 (2007):830–837.

2. Food and Nutrition Information Center, "The Dietary Reference Intakes (DRI) list more than 40 nutrients," United States Department of Agriculture, http://fnic.nal. usda.gov/nal_display/index.php?info_center=4&tax_level=1&tax_subject=242 (accessed August 2, 2007).

3. Harvard School of Public Health, "Protein: Moving Closer to Center Stage" Fact Sheet, Harvard University, http://www.hsph.harvard.edu/nutritionsource/protein. html (accessed August 2, 2007).

4. Jennifer J. Otten, Jennifer P., Hellwig, Linda D. Meyers, eds., *The Dietary Reference Intakes: The Essential Guide to Nutrient Requirements.* (Washington, D.C.: The National Academies Press, 2006), 145, 147.

Chapter 7

1. R.R. Pate, M. Pratt, S.N. Blair, W.L. Haskell, C.A. Macera, C. Bouchard, et al., "Physical activity and public health: a recommendation from the Centers for Disease Control and Prevention and the American College of Sports Medicine," *Journal of the American Medical Association* 273 (1995):402–407.

Chapter 8

1. R.B. Williams, et al., "Prognostic Importance of Social and Economic Resources among Medically Treated Patients with Angiographically Documented Coronary Artery Disease," *Journal of the American Medical Association* 267, no. 4 (1992): 520–4.

2. Janet Kornblum, "Study: 25% of Americans have no one to confide in," USA Today, June 22, 2006, http://www.usatoday.com/news/nation/2006-06-22-friendship_x. htm, Referencing a study co-authored by Lynn Smith Lovin of Duke University in *American Sociological Review* (accessed August 4, 2007).

3. Gene J. Koprowski, "Non-Profit Board Work Can Boost Your Career" CareerJournal. com, http://www.careerjournal.com/jobhunting/strategies/20030224-koprowski. html (accessed October 16, 2007).

4. Hans Selye, The Stress of Life (New York: McGraw-Hill, 1956).

5. S. Cohen, "The Pittsburgh common cold studies: psychosocial predictors of susceptibility to respiratory infectious illness," Keynote presentation at the Eight International Congress of Behavioral Medicine, Int J Behav Med. 12, no. 3 (2005):123-31.

6. National Institute for Occupational Health and Safety, "Stress . . . at Work," NIOSH Publication No 99-101, http://www.cdc.gov/niosh/stresswk.html (accessed on October 17, 2007)

7. National Center on Sleep Disorders Research, "Insomnia: Assessment and Management in Primary Care," http://www.nhlbi.nih.gov/about/ncsdr (accessed on October 2006).

8. Viktor Frankl, Man's Search for Meaning (New York: Beacon Press, 1959).

9. Henri Nouwen, The Return of the Prodigal Son (Darton, Longman & Todd Ltd, 1992).

10. Weight Control Information Network of NIDDK, "Prevalence Statistics Related to Overweight and Obesity," National Institute of Health, http://win.niddk.nih.gov/statistics/index.htm#preval (accessed October 17, 2007).

11. Table 3 Prevalence of BMI Levels in 1999–2002 (From NHANES 1999–2000), by Age Group in KM Flegel, et.al., "Excess Deaths Associated with Underweight, Overweight, and Obesity." *Journal of the American Medical Association* 293, no. 15 (2007).

12. John Farquhar and Gene Spiller, *The Last Puff* (New York: W.W. Norton and Company, 1991).